The Essentials of Edexcel GCSE Science is matched to the **Edexcel GCSE in Science specification (2101)**, based on the Key Stage 4 Programme of Study for Science. It provides full coverage of the three units: **Biology 1, Chemistry 1 and Physics 1**, and pages are **colour-coded** so that you can distinguish between them easily.

The content for each unit is divided into four **topics** to correspond with the specification and provide a clear, manageable structure to your revision.

At the end of each topic there is a **glossary of key words**. These pages can be used as checklists to help you with your revision. Make sure you are familiar with all the words listed and understand their meanings and relevance – they are central to your understanding of that topic!

How Science Works is an important new requirement in the Criteria for GCSE Science. It is a set of key concepts, relevant to all areas of science, concerned with the practices and procedures used to collect scientific evidence and the impact it has on society and your life. To reflect Edexcel's approach to How Science Works, and the way this element is taught in schools, these concepts are **integrated** with the scientific content throughout this guide.

As a revision guide, this book focuses on the material which is externally assessed (i.e. tested under exam conditions). It does not cover the practical skills assessment and assessment activities, which are marked by your teacher.

You will have to sit six **multiple-choice tests**, which each count for 10% of your final mark (60% in total). There are two tests per unit, each covering a pair of topics. The **contents list** in this revision guide clearly identifies these topic pairs, so that you can prepare for each paper individually.

This guide can be used to revise for either the **Foundation** or **Higher Tier** papers.

HT The material that is [...] enclosed in a coloured box, and can be easily identified by the symbol **HT** *.

At the end of the book, you will find a detailed **periodic table** which will provide a useful reference when you are studying the chemistry unit.

Spellings within this guide may differ from the British standard. This is deliberate, to ensure that spellings correspond with those on the specification and reflect those that will appear on your test papers.

Don't just read the information in this guide – **learn actively!** Jot down anything you think will help you to remember, no matter how trivial it may seem, and constantly test yourself without looking at the text.

Good luck with your exams!

Information About the Authors

Aleksander Jedrosz (Biology) is an experienced GCSE science teacher and examiner, currently working as a Curriculum Coordinator for the Sciences at a city academy. He is already the author of a book about the human eye.

Susan Loxley (Chemistry) has an excellent understanding of the applications of science in industry, having been involved in the development of materials for aerospace for 8 years. She now teaches chemistry to KS3 and KS4 pupils and is an examiner for GCSE science.

John Watts (Physics) was a physics teacher with over 25 years experience, and Head of Physics and Science at a northern comprehensive, before becoming a science consultant for an LA. He is currently working closely with city schools to help implement the new specifications.

*Higher tier material correct at time of going to print.

Contents

Contents

Environment

Food Chains

A **food chain** describes the feeding relationship between living organisms in a habitat. It also shows how energy and **biomass** are transferred along the food chain when the organisms feed.

Biomass refers to the total mass (quantity) of organic material at each stage in the chain, not the number of organisms.

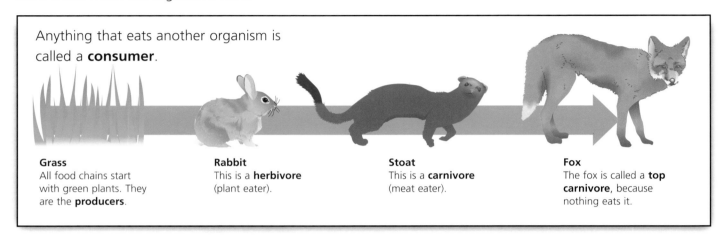

Anything that eats another organism is called a **consumer**.

Grass
All food chains start with green plants. They are the **producers**.

Rabbit
This is a **herbivore** (plant eater).

Stoat
This is a **carnivore** (meat eater).

Fox
The fox is called a **top carnivore**, because nothing eats it.

Pyramids of Biomass

Energy enters a food chain from the Sun. Some energy and biomass is lost at each stage of a food chain as...

- faeces (solid waste)
- movement energy
- heat energy (especially by birds and mammals).

Therefore, only a small amount of energy and biomass is incorporated into a consumer's body and transferred to the next feeding level. This is shown in a **pyramid of biomass**.

In the pyramid of biomass below, the loss of energy and biomass at each stage is indicated, and illustrates why such a representation of a food chain is always pyramid-shaped. This pyramid of biomass describes the food chain above quantitatively (amount of biomass).

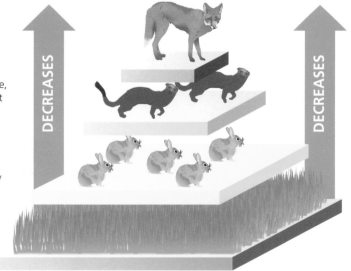

Energy

The fox gets the last tiny bit of energy left after all the others have had a share.

The stoats run around, mate, excrete, keep warm etc. and pass on about $\frac{1}{10}$ of all the energy they got from the rabbits.

The rabbits run around, mate, excrete, keep warm etc. and pass on about $\frac{1}{10}$ of all the energy they got from the grass.

The Sun is the energy source for all organisms, but only a fraction of the Sun's energy is actually captured in photosynthesis.

DECREASES

DECREASES

Biomass

The fox gets the biomass that remains to be passed on after all this!

The stoats lose quite a bit of biomass in droppings and urine.

The rabbits lose quite a lot of biomass in droppings and urine.

A lot of the biomass remains in the ground as the root system.

How Food Chains Affect Us

It is a lot more expensive to buy a sirloin steak than a loaf of bread at the supermarket.

This is because the main ingredient of bread is wheat flour, and wheat is a **producer**. About 10% of the light energy it absorbs is converted into food.

Beef steak comes from a cow, which is a **consumer**. Only 4% of the energy and biomass in the grass eaten by a cow is incorporated into the cow's body, i.e. converted into beef.

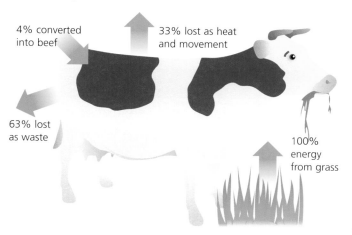

4% converted into beef

33% lost as heat and movement

63% lost as waste

100% energy from grass

This means a large amount of grass is needed to provide enough energy to support just two cows. However, if a farmer used the same land to produce wheat he could produce 9.5 tonnes of grain! This difference is reflected in the price of steak and bread.

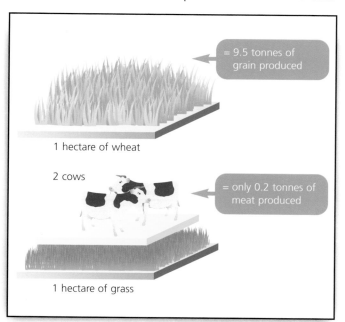

= 9.5 tonnes of grain produced

1 hectare of wheat

2 cows

= only 0.2 tonnes of meat produced

1 hectare of grass

Competition

Organisms in an **ecosystem** compete with each other for **space, food** and **water**.

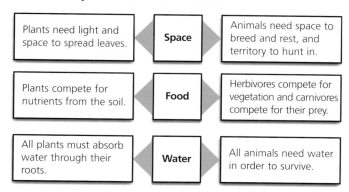

	Space	
Plants need light and space to spread leaves.	Space	Animals need space to breed and rest, and territory to hunt in.
Plants compete for nutrients from the soil.	Food	Herbivores compete for vegetation and carnivores compete for their prey.
All plants must absorb water through their roots.	Water	All animals need water in order to survive.

The plants and animals that are best **adapted** to their environment are most likely to be successful. For example…

- plants with deeper roots have access to water and nutrients that other plants cannot reach
- the animal with the strongest legs is most likely to catch the prey.

These successful organisms will often exist in larger numbers and may eventually out-compete other species, i.e. take over a particular habitat, gradually forcing other species to die out or move away.

If there is plenty of food and water a **population** will grow. However, it will eventually reach a size where **overcrowding** leads to disease and **competition** within the same species, so the numbers will fall dramatically:

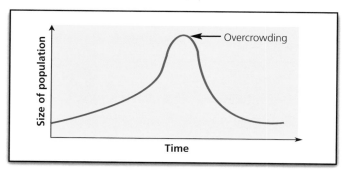

Intra-species Competition

Intra-species competition is when members of the same species compete for a resource; the strongest, healthiest and best adapted of the species will have a better chance of survival.

Environment

Predator–Prey Cycles

Predators are animals that kill and eat other animals, called **prey**. In natural habitats there is always a balance between the size of the predator population and the size of the prey population: there is **interdependence** between them.

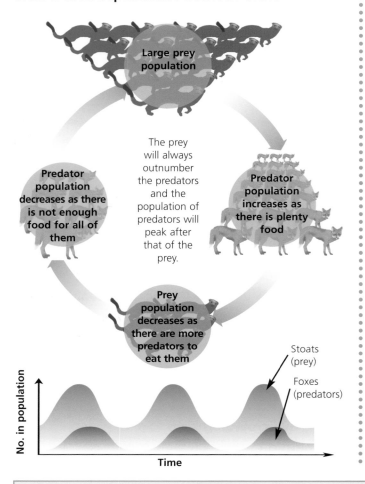

The prey will always outnumber the predators and the population of predators will peak after that of the prey.

Large prey population

Predator population increases as there is plenty food

Prey population decreases as there are more predators to eat them

Predator population decreases as there is not enough food for all of them

Stoats (prey)

Foxes (predators)

No. in population

Time

Computer Models of Populations

Scientists use **computer models** to estimate the size of a population. They look at a sample of the population and enter data about…

- life expectancy of the organism
- reproductive rate
- food availability
- size of habitat
- predators
- other factors that affect the organism.

By changing the data entered, scientists can use the model to predict what would happen to the size of the population in different scenarios.

Advantages
• Scientists can model a population over many generations in just a few minutes.   • Predictions can be made about the effects of factors like climate change or disease on a population.
Disadvantages
• Too many assumptions are made about the factors that affect a population's growth.   • A large number of factors which affect the size of natural populations must be programmed into the computer.

HT Human Activity

Human activity, e.g. farming, building and traffic, has a direct effect on the environment. For example, **sulphur dioxide** is a polluting gas produced when **fossil fuels** (e.g. coal) are burned.

Lichen populations are sensitive to sulphur dioxide levels; even low levels can kill them. This table shows how the quantity of lichens changes in relation to sulphur dioxide levels.

When human activity affects the population size of one species, it affects the whole food chain.

Distance (km) from an industrial town centre	Sulphur dioxide levels (arbitrary units)	Number of different lichens found
0	170	0
2	140	1
4	88	7
6	44	28
8	5	49
10	1	55

Changing Species

Over time, the characteristics of species can change.
There are three ways in which this can happen:

Method	Description	How it Happens
Natural Selection	The basis of **Darwin's Theory of Evolution**: individuals with characteristics that make them better suited / adapted to their environment are more likely to survive and reproduce.	Naturally
Select / Selective Breeding	Individuals with specific characteristics are selected and bred to produce offspring with desirable features.	Human intervention
Genetic Engineering	Genes (DNA) from one organism are implanted into another organism to introduce certain characteristics. Organisms can be of the same species or different species.	Human intervention

Select Breeding – Example

Farmers with livestock have been using the principles of select breeding for hundreds of years without fully understanding the genetic basis for it. The simple rule was to keep the best animals to breed from, and send the rest to market.

In a competitive farming industry, cattle need to be highly efficient if the farm is to make money. Efficiency means **specialisation**. For example, cattle are selectively bred for one of the following characteristics:

- beef production
- quality of milk produced
- quantity of milk produced, for example:

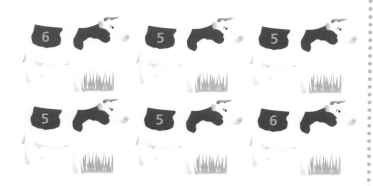

Most cows produce 5 gallons, two in the herd produce 6.
The two that produce 6 gallons are used to breed from.

Genetic Engineering – Example

Soya is a very important food: the beans contain lots of protein. Unfortunately, the growing conditions needed for soya also encourage weeds. Herbicides used to kill weeds would normally kill the soya plants too. However, soya has been **genetically modified** to resist glyphosate (the chemical in herbicides) by the following process:

1. A glyphosate-resistant weed is found.
2. The gene responsible for the resistance is identified.
3. The gene is cut out using a special enzyme.
4. The gene is transferred to the embryo soya plants.
5. As they grow, the plants are sprayed with glyphosate herbicide to test them.
6. If the gene transplant is successful the soya plants will survive.
7. They are now GM (genetically modified) plants.

Environment

Farming Methods

Intensive farming uses methods that yield high volumes of eggs, crops and meat.

Other farmers use **organic** principles to produce food. These principles include…

- having respect for their animals
- producing as little pollution as possible
- not using artificial (chemical) fertilisers and pesticides
- being sustainable.

Organic products usually cost more. Here's why:

Intensive Farms	Organic Farms
Cost a lot to set up	Cost less to set up but more to run
Specialise in one product	Balance various different crops and livestock
Use lots of chemical fertilisers and pesticides which are cost effective	Use organic fertilisers (dung) which are more costly
Need less space	Need more space to produce the same volumes
Not labour intensive – a lot of the work is done by machines	Very labour intensive – most of the work is done manually

> **Genetic Modification, GM,** (see Genetic Engineering p.7) can be used in intensive farming to make the crop plants…
> - herbicide resistant, e.g. soya and maize
> - have a longer shelf-life, e.g. tomatoes
> - more appealing to consumers (i.e. a favourable colour, shape or flavour).

Evolution

The theory of **evolution** states that all living organisms alive today (and those that are now **extinct**) developed from simple life forms.

To survive, species **evolve** to become better adapted to their environment. Species that are less well-adapted may become extinct.

> **Charles Darwin** (1809–1882) was a naturalist who made four very important observations:
>
> - All living things produce more offspring than survive to adulthood.
> - Populations remain more or less constant in numbers.
> - Members of the same species show variation (they are not all identical).
> - Many features are inherited (passed on from parent to offspring over generations).
>
> He deduced that all organisms are involved in a struggle for survival and that only the best-adapted survive. Organisms that survive are more likely to reproduce and pass their (well-adapted) genes on to their offspring. The rest die out. So, very gradually, a species will change. This formed the basis of Darwin's theory of **Evolution by Natural Selection**.
>
> At first Darwin had great difficulty in having his theory accepted because it is difficult to prove, and many scientists did not (and some still do not) accept the theory. Most rejected it because it contradicted the Bible. (In those days the Church had great influence over what people thought).
>
> Alfred Russel Wallace (1823-1913) was another naturalist with similar ideas to Darwin.

Environment

The Fossil Record

Fossils are the remains of living organisms from millions of years ago, found in **sedimentary rocks**. They provide evidence of how organisms have evolved. However, the fossil record is incomplete because...

- some body parts do not fossilise (the soft bits decay)
- many living organisms do not have hard parts that can be fossilised
- many fossils have not yet been discovered.

Despite this, these gradual changes confirm that species have changed over long periods of time, providing strong evidence for evolution.

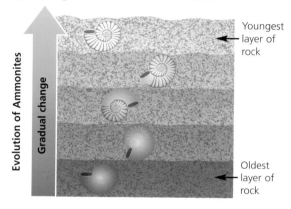

Natural Selection

Over generations, evolution produces changes in a species and can even lead to the formation of **new species**:

1. Individuals in a population show **variation** (differences).
2. Individuals in a population are killed due to **predation** and **competition** for food, a mate and space.
3. Individuals that are better adapted will survive, breed and produce offspring. This is called **survival of the fittest**.
4. The survivors **pass on their genes** to their offspring.
5. Over **successive generations**, better adapted individuals become more common within a population.

Organisms that are not well-adapted to their environment could become **extinct**.

Natural Selection – Example

The **Peppered Moth** was originally pale and speckled in colour. This meant they were camouflaged against the bark of silver birch trees, so predators (birds) found it difficult to see them.

During the industrial revolution (about 200 years ago) the air became polluted from factories and mills, and silver birch trees became black with soot. At this time, natural selection led to a new variety of Peppered Moth.

Peppered Moth

Black Peppered Moth

1. **Variation:** a Peppered Moth that was black in colour occurred as the result of a genetic mutation.
2. **Competition:** the new black moths had to compete with the pale, speckled variety for mates, space, water, and to avoid **predation**.
3. **Better adapted:** the black Peppered Moths were eaten less often in polluted areas as they were camouflaged against the black bark of trees. Pale moths were easily seen and were eaten.
4. **Pass on their genes:** the dark-coloured moths survived and bred, passing on their genes.
5. **Successive generations:** as time passed the number of black moths found in polluted areas increased.

In the mid-1950s the Government passed the Clean Air Act. This dramatically reduced air pollution and so more silver birch trees stayed 'silver'. This meant that the pale variety of moth had an advantage again and so, due to natural selection, began to grow in numbers. Today, the presence of the pale variety of Peppered Moth is regarded as a marker for clean air.

Environment

Classification

There are millions of different organisms and species and they are all **classified** (grouped) on the basis of their similarities and differences.

There are five groups which are called **kingdoms**: plants, animals, fungi, protoctists and prokaryotes (see below). These kingdoms can then be divided into smaller groups. For example, the table below right shows how the animal kingdom can be divided into **vertebrates** (animals with backbones) and **invertebrates** (animals without backbones). They are then classified in smaller, even more specific groups.

Usually an organism will clearly fit into a group, but occasionally there are exceptions. For example, the duck-billed platypus has fur but it also has a bill and lays eggs – so is it a mammal or a bird?

Kingdoms
Plants
• they have cellulose cell walls • they photosynthesise
Animals
• they have a nervous system
Fungi
• they do not contain chlorophyll
Protoctists (mostly single cells)
• they do not have specialised cells
Prokaryotes (bacteria)
• they have no nucleus

Vertebrates	Invertebrates
Fish	**Annelids**
John Dory fish	Earthworm
Amphibians	**Molluscs**
Frog	Mussel
Reptiles	**Crustaceans**
Snake	Woodlouse
Birds	**Arachnids**
Skylark	Scorpion
Mammals	**Insects**
Sheep	Beetle

Glossary

Adaptation – a change or adjustment which improves an organism's ability to survive and reproduce in a given environment

Biomass – the total mass of organic material (no water) of an organism or population

Breeding – reproduction of animals and plants (often using parents with desirable qualities, which will be passed to the offspring: select breeding)

Characteristics – features that an organism has. These can be either unique to a species or unique to a larger group

Classification – groups into which all living things are placed according to their characteristics. The main groups are called kingdoms (there are five of these). The smallest subdivision is a species (there are millions of these)

Competition – occurs when different species, or members of the same species, need the same resources to survive

Ecosystem – refers to all the plants and animals in a particular environment, and their relationships with each other and their environment

Environment – the area in which an organism lives or exists

Evolution – the changes that take place in a species over a very long period of time, which result in the species being better adapted for survival

Extinct – when a species completely dies out and there are no more individuals left

Food chain – the order in which energy and biomass are transferred from one organism to the next, by being eaten. A chain always starts with a producer (green plant)

Fossil – the remains of an organism preserved in rock

Genetic engineering – the technology that involves moving genes (DNA) from one organism to another. It can be within species or between species

Genetically modified – an organism that has had new genes introduced to its original genetic make-up through genetic engineering. GMO – genetically modified organism

Interdependence – where the population number of an organism depends on the population number of another organism

Intra-species – between members of the same species (often relates to competition)

Natural selection – the survival of individual organisms which are best suited / adapted to their environment (the basis of Darwin's Theory of Evolution)

Organic – natural, of plant or animal origin

Organism – any living thing (i.e. anything that performs the seven features of living things: movement, nutrition, respiration, excretion, growth, reproduction and response)

Population – all the members of a species living in a defined area

Predator – a creature that hunts and kills other creatures for food

Prey – a creature that is hunted by other creatures for food

Quantitatively – refers to amounts (opposed to qualitative, which refers to appearances)

Reproduction – the process of living organisms producing offspring

Species – a class of related, living organisms which are able to breed and produce fertile offspring

Variation – differences between individuals of the same species

Genes

Chromosomes, Genes and DNA

In the nucleus of a normal human body cell there are two sets of **chromosomes**. One set comes from the mother and the other from the father. Each set consists of 23 individual chromosomes. So each cell has 46 chromosomes (23 pairs) in total.

Chromosomes are divided into sections called **genes**. It is the genes that control how our cells function and what characteristics we have.

Chromosomes (and therefore genes) are made of a chemical called **DNA**. The DNA molecule consists of two strands which are coiled around each other to form a **double helix**.

Special chemicals called **bases** protrude (stick out) from each strand of the DNA molecules. They are joined together in the middle so that the DNA molecule looks like a twisted ladder.

There are four bases: **adenine** (A); **cytosine** (C); **guanine** (G) and **thymine** (T). The bases from the two strands pair up in a precise way:

* A links with T
* C links with G.

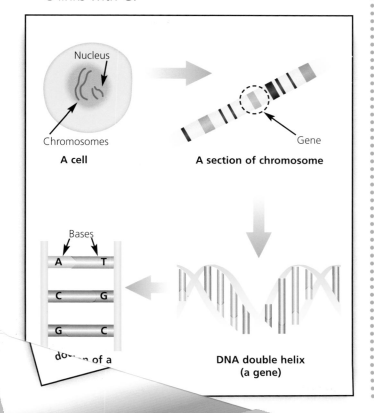

Nucleus

Chromosomes

A cell

Gene

A section of chromosome

Bases

A   T

C   G

G   C

do...n of a

DNA double helix
(a gene)

The Human Genome Project

In 1977, a scientist called Fred Sanger discovered a way of identifying the sequences of bases in DNA.

A **genome** refers to all the genetic material in an organism, and the **Human Genome Project**, completed in 2000, used Sanger's method to identify the sequence of bases in every gene that appears on human chromosomes (30 000) – that is millions of base pairs!

Knowing where a gene appears on a chromosome and how it is made up could be very useful. For example, doctors could identify and replace 'faulty' genes which cause disorders (see p.13); forensic scientists could use the information to compare DNA samples from potential suspects to those found at a crime scene, and convict or clear them of the crime.

But the question still remains: should scientists have done this work? There are concerns that the information could be misused and concerns over who will have access to the information. And, of course, mistakes could be made.

Ⓗ Transgenic Animals

A **transgenic animal** is one whose genome has had a gene, or genes, transferred to it from another organism of a different species. It will have been **genetically modified** (GM).

For example, transgenic cows have been created to produce 'designer milk' which contains…

* extra protein (milk protein is known as casein)
* low levels of cholesterol
* human antibodies (normally produced by our white blood cells).

So transgenic animals, like these cows, have enormous potential. They could be 'designed' to produce all sorts of things that humans need for good health and development.

Gene Therapy

The aim of **gene therapy** is to treat disease and disorders by modifying a person's genome.

It is impossible to change the genes in every cell but, by targeting specific areas, it is possible to provide some degree of cure. This is particularly true for conditions caused by two recessive alleles, like cystic fibrosis.

Viruses are used as vectors, i.e. to deliver genetic material to the target cells. These viruses have been modified so they cannot multiply and cause disease.

Treating Diseases Genetically

Cystic Fibrosis

Cystic fibrosis is an inherited disease that affects cell membranes. It is caused by a recessive gene (see p.16) so it has to be inherited from both parents.

Characteristics of the disease include…
- being unable to digest food properly
- airways becoming clogged with excess, sticky mucus
- chest infections, including pneumonia
- shorter life expectancy – sufferers often die aged between 40 and 50.

A girl with cystic fibrosis using an inhaler

There is no cure for cystic fibrosis, but the symptoms can be treated. Sufferers are given enzyme tablets, chest physiotherapy, and antibiotics for chest infections.

The condition can also be treated by gene therapy. This is how it works:

> The patient is anaesthetised.

> Whilst asleep they inhale the vector virus carrying the 'normal genes' through an aerosol.

> Some of these 'normal genes' enter lung cells.

> Patients feel much better for about four weeks.

Although gene therapy can be very effective, it is very expensive and the effects are only short-term.

Breast Cancer

Gene therapy also has the potential to be used for treating breast cancer.

Scientists have discovered specific genes that, if present, increase the chance of a woman developing breast cancer. Removing these problem genes and replacing them with normal, healthy genes would eliminate this risk. However, the problem genes would need to be removed from every cell. The only way this can be achieved is to identify and replace the genes when the woman is first conceived, i.e. is a fertilised egg, and the cells have yet to multiply.

Genes

Sexual Reproduction

During **fertilisation**, **gametes** (i.e. a **sperm** cell from the father and an **egg** cell from the mother) fuse together, so the offspring gets half its genes from each parent. This means that the offspring will inherit characteristics from both parents, leading to **variation** (differences between individuals).

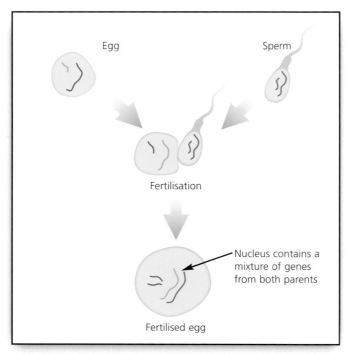

Asexual Reproduction

The offspring produced by **asexual reproduction** get their genes from one parent only. So they have exactly the same genes as the parent. This makes them **clones**.

It is possible for plants to reproduce asexually (i.e. without flowers or fertilisation). For example, the Chlorophytum (spider plant) throws off **runners**:

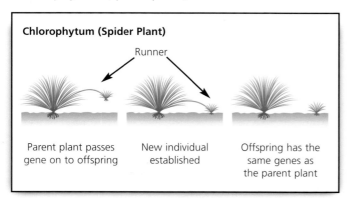

Clones

Clones are individuals which are genetically identical. Identical twins and triplets are natural clones as they have exactly the same genes and chromosomes.

It is possible to make clones artificially. In 1996, Dolly the sheep was the first cloned mammal. Since then, lots of mammals have been produced by cloning techniques, including dogs and cats.

It is also possible, using tissue culture techniques, to clone tissues and organs for transplant surgery.

However, scientists, as well as the general public, have social and ethical concerns with cloning mammals and human body parts.

Some people think that cloning is the inevitable result of scientific progress and we should be allowed to benefit from it. However, others believe that we should not tamper with nature. Some concerns about cloning include…

* the fear of creating the 'perfect race'
* the possibilities of abnormalities occurring in clones
* clones will not have 'parents'
* cloning does not allow 'natural' evolution.

'Designer Babies'

Scientific advances allow doctors and parents to test unborn embryos for genetic disorders and diseases, meaning healthy embryos can be selected. However, people are worried that in the future we will also be able to select embryos on the basis of sex and cosmetic features, resulting in a generation of **'designer babies'**.

Many people feel that letting parents 'choose' their child's sex and features is against 'nature's way', or even against 'God's will'. As a result, doctors and scientists are finding it difficult for such scientific advances to be accepted.

N.B. 'Designer babies' is a term used by the media, not by scientists or doctors.

Variation

Variation is due to two factors:

1 **Genetic causes (inheritance):** variation due to the genes inherited by an individual.

2 **Environmental causes:** variation due to the conditions in which an individual has developed.

Inheritance v Environment (Nature v Nurture)

There has been a long and lively debate over the relative importance of genetic and environmental factors in determining certain characteristics. Most people now agree that variation is due to a combination of genetic and environmental causes. The table opposite illustrates this.

Feature	Genetic factors	Environmental factors
Sporting ability	• a person's natural sporting ability and co-ordination • natural physique and body structure	• good coaching • positive support • excellent facilities and opportunities to practise
Intelligence	• the structure of the brain and its nerve connections	• support from home • quality of education • life experience

Factors Affecting Growth

The size of an organism is determined by a combination of genes. However, environmental factors can also affect the overall outcome.

This graph shows the effect of the mother's diet (in terms of energy intake) on the birth weight of her baby. It shows that mothers who take in more energy have larger babies.

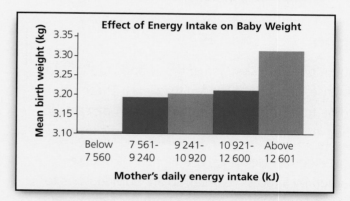

Effect of Energy Intake on Baby Weight

Mean birth weight (kg) on y-axis: 3.10, 3.15, 3.20, 3.25, 3.30, 3.35

Mother's daily energy intake (kJ) on x-axis: Below 7 560, 7 561–9 240, 9 241–10 920, 10 921–12 600, Above 12 601

Minerals and Growth in Plants

The genes that plants inherit will give them the potential to grow properly. However, to fulfil this potential, plants need certain minerals which they absorb through their roots.

If the environment lacks the minerals a plant needs, even though it has the right genes, it will not grow properly.

Lack of phosphates   Lack of potassium

Mineral resource	Why it is needed	Effect of deficiency
Nitrates	• to make proteins for growth	• stunted growth • older leaves turn yellow
Phosphates	• important in respiration • important in photosynthesis • to make proteins	• poor root growth • small leaves
Potassium	• to help the enzymes involved in respiration and photosynthesis to work properly	• yellow leaves with dead patches
Magnesium	• to make chlorophyll	• yellow leaves

Genes

Alleles

A gene is the part of a chromosome that controls the development of a characteristic, either individually or in combination with other associated genes. For each gene, there can be different versions called **alleles**.

As we already know, normal body cells (not gametes) contain pairs of chromosomes. This means that genes also exist in pairs; one on each chromosome. So, for each gene an individual might have two matching alleles or two different alleles.

A **dominant allele** is an allele that controls the development of a characteristic, even when it is only present on one of the chromosomes in a pair.

A **recessive allele** only controls the development of a characteristic if it is present on both of the chromosomes in a pair.

Inherited Diseases

Some diseases, like cystic fibrosis and Huntington's disease, are caused by 'faulty' alleles. These can come from the mother, father or both parents, so they are called **inherited** or **genetic diseases**.

Cystic fibrosis (see p.13) is an inherited disease caused by a recessive allele, so an individual has to inherit two faulty alleles (one from the father and one from the mother) to have the disease. Individuals who have only one faulty allele will not have the disease. However, the faulty allele could be passed on to their offspring, so these individuals are **carriers**.

Huntington's disease affects the nervous system. It is caused by a dominant allele, so an individual only has to inherit one faulty allele (from the mother or father) to have the disease.

Capital letter = dominant allele. Small letter = recessive allele.

H ⟷ **Huntington's Disease** One dominant allele and one recessive allele, therefore has Huntington's disease. ⟷ h

HT Genetic Variation

For each pair of genes there are several possible combinations of alleles, which produce different outcomes.

For example…
- the gene that controls tongue rolling has two alleles: one for the ability to roll the tongue and one for being unable to roll the tongue
- the gene that controls earlobe type has two alleles: one for attached earlobes and one for unattached earlobes.

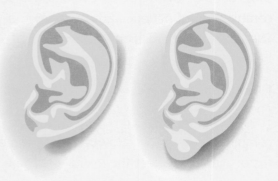

Attached earlobe   Unattached earlobe

When both alleles are dominant, the individual is described as being **homozygous dominant** for that gene or condition.

When both alleles are recessive, the individual is described as being **homozygous recessive** for that gene or condition.

When there is one dominant allele and one recessive allele, the individual is described as being **heterozygous** for that gene or condition.

So, the possible combinations are as follows:

	Homozygous dominant	Heterozygous	Homozygous recessive
Earlobes	EE (free lobes)	Ee (free lobes)	ee (attached lobes)
Tongue rolling	TT (can roll)	Tt (can roll)	tt (cannot roll)

ⓣ Inheritance

When a characteristic is determined by just one pair of alleles then simple genetic crosses can be performed to investigate the mechanism of inheritance. These simple crosses are examples of **monohybrid inheritance**.

These crosses can be shown using two types of genetic diagram: a grid (as in examples ❶, ❸ and ❹) or as a family-tree type diagram (as in example ❷).

In all genetic diagrams we use capital letters for dominant alleles and lower case letters for recessive alleles. In tongue rolling, therefore, we use T for being able to tongue roll and t for not being able to tongue roll.

Opposite are typical examples you may be asked about in your exam. So remember to…
- clearly identify the alleles of the parents
- separate each pair of alleles into individual gametes
- show all possible combinations, i.e. each gamete from the father should be paired with each gamete from the mother in turn.

In diagrams ❶ and ❷ opposite, one parent has two dominant genes, so each offspring will inherit the dominant feature. In diagram ❸ each parent has one dominant allele and one recessive allele, so each offspring will have a 3 in 4 (75%) chance of inheriting the dominant feature. In diagram ❹ one parent has one recessive allele and the other parent has two recessive alleles, so each offspring will have a 1 in 2 (50%) chance of inheriting the dominant feature.

The possible outcomes for one pair of alleles are limited, but there are numerous genes on the chromosomes in human body cells. This is why individuals of the same species (even brothers and sisters) show variation; because there are so many different combinations possible.

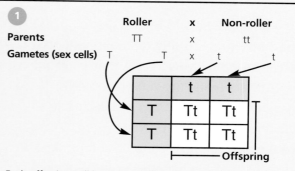

Each offspring will be able to roll their tongue (because the dominant allele is present in each cross).

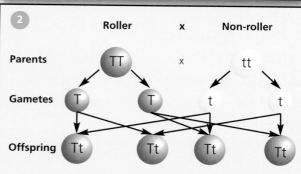

Same as above. Each offspring will be able to roll their tongue (because the dominant allele is present in each cross).

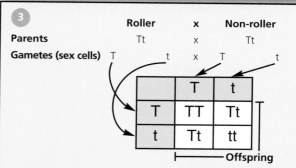

Each offspring has a 3 in 4 chance of being able to roll their tongue (because the dominant allele is present in three out of four crosses).

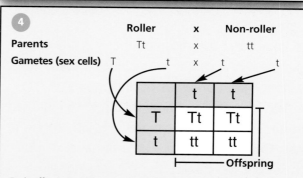

Each offspring will have a 1 in 2 chance of being able to roll their tongue (because the dominant allele is present in half the crosses).

Genes

Glossary

Allele – an alternative form of a gene

Antibodies – proteins that neutralise antigens (chemicals made by foreign cells that enter the body). They are made by white blood cells. There are many different antibodies and each one is specific for a different antigen

Asexual reproduction – a form of reproduction that does not involve gametes or fertilisation. The offspring are genetically identical to the parents (the offspring are clones)

Cancer – a disease which causes cells to divide uncontrollably to form tumours

Cell – basic unit of life

Characteristic – a feature that an individual has

Chromosome – composed of DNA and protein; consists of a series of genes

Clone – an individual that is genetically identical to its parent

Cystic fibrosis – a disease inherited as the result of a recessive gene, which affects the cell membranes

DNA (deoxyribonucleic acid) – substance from which chromosomes are made

Dominant – the stronger allele in a pair

Environment – the area in which an organism lives or exists (a complex, multicellular organism will have an internal environment as well as an external one)

Fertilisation – the joining together of an egg with a sperm during sexual reproduction

Forensic – using science to solve crimes, e.g. genetic fingerprinting

Gametes – sex cells (sperm and ova / eggs)

Gene – part of a chromosome that controls the development of a characteristic individually or in combination with other, associated genes

Genetics – the study of how features are inherited

Genome – all the genetic material of an organism

Human Genome Project – an international project which set out to establish the sequence of all the bases in the genes of all 23 pairs of human chromosomes

Inheritance – how features are passed on through reproduction

Nucleus – the part of a cell which is surrounded by a membrane and contains the chromosomes

Recessive – the weaker allele of a pair

Sexual reproduction – a form of reproduction that involves the fusion of an egg with a sperm during fertilisation

Transplant – the transfer of an organ from one person to another

Variation – the differences between organisms of the same species

---

HT **Generation** – a group of genetically related individuals who represent a single stage in descent, e.g. grandfather, father and son are three generations; the act of producing (generating) offspring

Transgenic – an organism whose genome has received a gene or genes from another organism

---

Electrical and Chemical Signals

The Nervous System

The **nervous system** consists of the **brain**, the **spinal cord** and paired **nerves** and **receptors** (sense organs). The brain and the spinal cord are referred to together as the **central nervous system** (CNS).

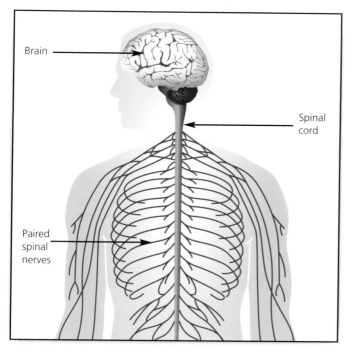

The nervous system allows organisms to react to their surroundings and coordinate their behaviour.

Humans have five senses. Receptors in the sense organs detect internal and external changes, allowing the body to respond to these stimuli:

- sight (eyes)
- hearing (ears)
- taste (taste buds on the tongue)
- smell (chemical receptors in the nose)
- touch (receptors in the skin).

N.B. Balance (ears) may also be referred to as a sense.

Information from the receptors passes along neurones (nerve cells) to the brain, which coordinates the response.

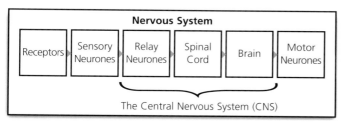

The Brain

The **brain** coordinates most of the actions of the body. It has three main parts:

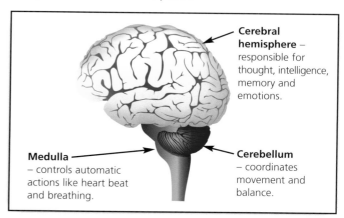

(HT) Disruption to the Brain

The brain is the most delicate organ in the human body. It receives, stores and recalls information, and instructs and coordinates actions. But sometimes things go wrong:

Tumours develop when cells in the brain divide and grow uncontrollably. The tumour presses against other parts of the brain, which results in them not working properly.

Parkinson's Disease develops when the brain stops producing dopamine, a chemical that brain cells use to communicate with each other. A lack of dopamine means the brain cannot coordinate the movements of the body properly (amongst other things).

Strokes happen when part of the brain is starved of oxygen and stops working properly. For example, if the affected part coordinates speech, then the sufferer will not be able to speak properly after the stroke.

Grand Mal Epilepsy: brain neurones communicate with each other by sending electrical impulses. Sometimes these impulses are random; the brain sends out uncoordinated instructions to the body, thus causing epileptic fits.

Electrical and Chemical Signals

Neurones

Neurones are specially-adapted cells that carry electrical signals called **impulses**. Neurones are elongated (stretched out) to make connections between parts of the body. They have branched endings which allow a single neurone to act on many muscle fibres or connect with many other neurones. There are three types of neurone:

1. **Sensory neurones:** these take nerve impulses from the sense organs (receptors) to the central nervous system.

Direction of impulse (towards cell body).

2. **Relay neurones:** these pass impulses on from sensory neurones to motor neurones in the CNS.

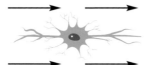

Impulse travels first towards, and then away from, cell body.

3. **Motor neurones:** these take impulses from the central nervous system to the muscles or glands.

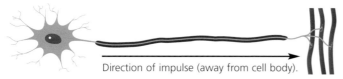

Direction of impulse (away from cell body).

Synapse

Neurones pass information into and out of the central nervous system. Neurones do not touch each other. There is a very small gap between them called a **synapse** (see diagram top right).

1. When an electrical impulse reaches this gap via neurone A a chemical transmitter is released and activates receptors on Neurone B.
2. This causes an electrical impulse to be generated in Neurone B.
3. The chemical transmitter is then destroyed.

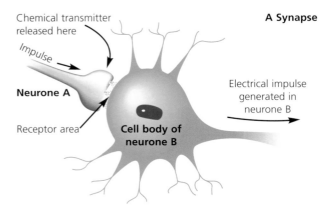

Chemical transmitter released here

Impulse

Neurone A

Receptor area

Cell body of neurone B

Electrical impulse generated in neurone B

A Synapse

So, an impulse will go along the following pathway:

| **Sense organ** |
| Receptors detect a change either inside or outside the body. This change is a stimulus. |

| **Sensory neurone** |
| Conducts the impulse from the sense organ towards the CNS. |

| **Synapse** |
| The gap between the sensory and relay neurones. |

| **Relay neurone** |
| Passes the impulse on to a motor neurone. |

| **Synapse** |
| The gap between the relay neurone and the motor neurone. |

| **Motor neurone** |
| Passes the impulse on to the muscle. |

| **Muscle** |
| The muscle will respond by contracting which results in a movement. |

Measuring Reaction Time

We all need to have fast reactions, but sometimes people need particularly quick ones, for example, when playing table tennis or driving a car.

You can measure your reaction time by catching a falling ruler. If you have very quick reactions you will catch the ruler near the end. If you have slower reactions, more of the ruler will fall before you catch it.

Electrical and Chemical Signals

Voluntary and Reflex Responses

Voluntary Responses (Actions)

These are actions over which we have complete control – we consciously decide to act. For example, speaking, walking or picking something up.

Stimulus	Receptors	Coordinator	Effectors	Response
Freshly baked cake	Sight and smell receptors	**Sensory Neurones** ▼ **CNS** ▼ **Motor Neurones** ▶	Muscles in hand	Move hand to pick up cake

Involuntary / Reflex Responses (Actions)

These are responses over which we have no control – they happen automatically. For example, blinking, pupil reflex or moving part of your body away from pain.

Stimulus	Receptors	Coordinator	Effectors	Response
Drawing pin	Pain receptor (in finger)	**Sensory Neurones** ▼ **Relay Neurone in Spinal Cord** ▼ **Motor Neurones** ▶	Muscles in hand	Withdraw hand

Reflex Arcs

Sometimes conscious action would be too slow to prevent harm to the body. Reflex action speeds up the response time by missing out the brain. The spinal cord acts as the coordinator and passes impulses directly from a sensory neurone to a motor neurone via a relay neurone which bypasses the brain. This is called a **reflex arc** (see diagram below).

1 A receptor is stimulated by the drawing pin (stimulus)...

2 ...causing impulses to pass along a sensory neurone into the spinal cord.

3 The sensory neurone synapses with a relay neurone.

4 The relay neurone synapses with a motor neurone, bypassing the brain and sending impulses down the motor neurone...

5 ...to the muscles (effectors) causing them to contract in response to the sharp drawing pin.

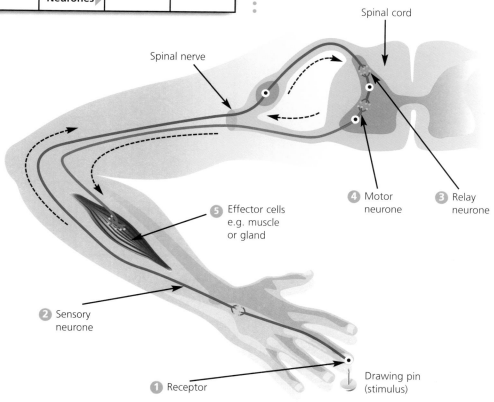

Spinal cord

Spinal nerve

4 Motor neurone

3 Relay neurone

5 Effector cells e.g. muscle or gland

2 Sensory neurone

1 Receptor

Drawing pin (stimulus)

Electrical and Chemical Signals

Examples of Reflex Actions

Example 1 – Accommodation

The eye is a complicated sense organ which focuses light onto light-sensitive receptor cells in the retina. These are stimulated, causing nerve impulses to pass along sensory neurones to the brain.

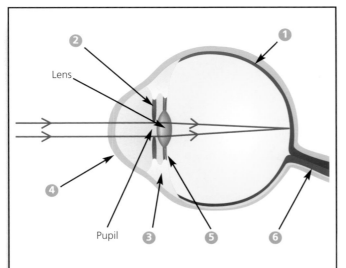

1. Retina – contains the receptor cells which are sensitive to light
2. Iris – coloured part, made of muscle, controls amount of light entering the eye
3. Ciliary body – muscle, controls the shape of the lens
4. Cornea – transparent part of sclera (the outer coat of the eyeball), refracts light
5. Suspensory ligament – holds lens in place
6. Optic nerve – carries impulses via sensory neurones to the brain

The cornea and the lens focus rays of light so that an image is formed on the retina. Rays of light are bent (refracted) by the cornea. The rays of light are then further refracted by the lens to produce a clear image on the retina.

Focusing on objects at different distances requires adjustments to be made, called **accommodation**.

To focus on a **distant object** the ciliary body relaxes and the suspensory ligaments pull tight. The lens is pulled 'thinner' and light is not bent as much.

To focus on a **near object** the ciliary body contracts. The suspensory ligaments go slack allowing the lens to become fatter so light is bent much more.

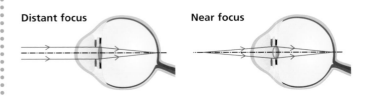

The fluid in the eye retains the shape of the eye and keeps the suspensory ligaments tight. The ciliary body has to work to overcome this tension which is why eyes get tired after lots of focusing on near objects, e.g. reading, or working at a computer monitor.

Example 2 – The Iris Reflex

The pupil of the human eye can increase and decrease in size in order to regulate the amount of light entering the eye.

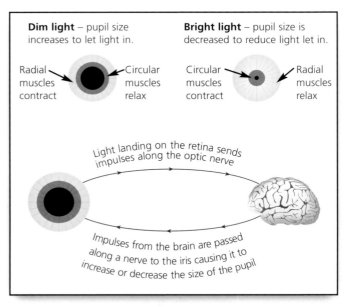

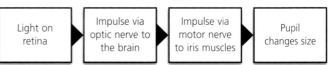

Example 3 – 'Ducking' Reaction

If you were walking along a country lane, and suddenly a bird swooped down low over your head, you would 'duck'. This is an automatic reaction to protect you from harm; you cannot help it as it is a reflex action: you do it without thinking.

Electrical and Chemical Signals

The Blood

Blood has four components:

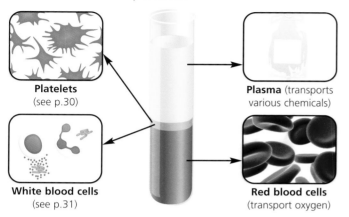

Platelets (see p.30)

White blood cells (see p.31)

Plasma (transports various chemicals)

Red blood cells (transport oxygen)

Red Blood Cells

- They have no nucleus so that they can be packed with **haemoglobin.**
- The bi-concave shape of the cells provides a bigger surface area through which to absorb oxygen.
- Haemoglobin combines easily with oxygen.
- In the lungs, where there is lots of oxygen, haemoglobin + oxygen → **oxyhaemoglobin.**
- In the tissues where oxygen is being used up, oxyhaemoglobin → haemoglobin + oxygen.
- Haemoglobin's reversible reaction with oxygen ensures oxygen is transported to where it is needed.

Plasma

Plasma is a straw-coloured liquid consisting mainly of water. It transports...

- carbon dioxide from the organs to the lungs
- soluble products of digestion (e.g. glucose and amino acids) from the small intestine
- urea from the liver to the kidneys
- chemical messengers called hormones
- water to and from various parts of the body.

Hormones and Coordination

Hormones are chemical messengers, produced by **endocrine glands**. Hormones coordinate and control the way in which parts of the body (target organs or target cells) function. Hormones are transported to their **target organs** or **target cells** through the bloodstream. For example...

- the pancreas produces **insulin**

- the adrenal glands (above the kidneys) produce **adrenaline**
- the pituitary gland (in the brain) produces a **growth hormone**, **FSH** and **LH**.
- in males the testes produce **testosterone**
- in females the ovaries produce **oestrogen** and **progesterone**, e.g:

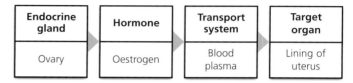

Endocrine gland	Hormone	Transport system	Target organ
Ovary	Oestrogen	Blood plasma	Lining of uterus

The Menstrual Cycle

Between the ages of approximately 13 and 50, a woman is fertile and the lining of her uterus is replaced every month in preparation to carry a baby. This is a period.

HT We can represent the changes in the **ovary**, the **uterus wall** and the level of hormones over the 28-day cycle like this:

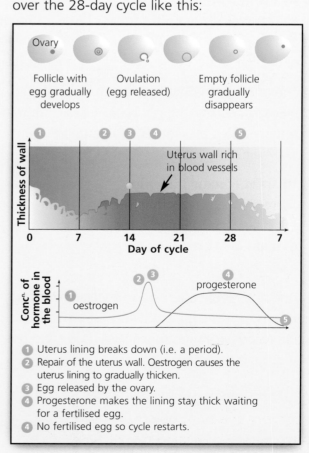

Ovary

Follicle with egg gradually develops

Ovulation (egg released)

Empty follicle gradually disappears

Uterus wall rich in blood vessels

oestrogen

progesterone

1. Uterus lining breaks down (i.e. a period).
2. Repair of the uterus wall. Oestrogen causes the uterus lining to gradually thicken.
3. Egg released by the ovary.
4. Progesterone makes the lining stay thick waiting for a fertilised egg.
4. No fertilised egg so cycle restarts.

Electrical and Chemical Signals

Natural Control of Fertility

- **Oestrogen** causes the lining of the uterus to thicken during the early part of the menstrual cycle, i.e. it repairs it after a period.
- **Progesterone** is produced after an egg is released. It preserves and maintains the uterus wall during the middle part of the cycle.
- If **fertilisation** occurs and a woman becomes pregnant then the ovary continues to produce progesterone until the placenta is formed. The placenta then produces progesterone for the remainder of the pregnancy, maintaining the uterus wall and preventing further ovulation.

Artificial Control of Fertility

It is possible to artificially produce the hormones oestrogen and progesterone to control fertility. Manufactured oestrogen and progesterone can be used in two ways:

1 As Contraception

The **contraceptive pill** contains both oestrogen and progesterone. This prevents the development of the eggs in the ovaries and subsequent ovulation.

The '**mini-pill**' contains progesterone. Though ovulation occurs, the cervix produces extra thick **mucus** which prevents sperm getting through to where the eggs are.

2 To Treat Female Infertility

There are many reasons why a woman may be **infertile**. One common cause is an inability to **ovulate** (a failure to release eggs). This is due to a lack of natural oestrogen.

About 90% of cases can be resolved by taking tablets containing a synthetic oestrogen. This raises the body's oestrogen levels and therefore triggers ovulation.

In-vitro Fertilisation (IVF)

Some couples are not able to conceive naturally, for example if the man does not produce enough sperm or if the woman's oviducts are blocked. **IVF** can sometimes help. The stages of IVF are as follows:

1. The doctor makes a small cut in the woman's abdomen and a thin tube is inserted; eggs are then removed.
2. The eggs are kept alive by placing them in a solution containing food and oxygen.
3. Semen (containing sperm) from the father is then mixed with the eggs in a glass dish.
4. The fertilised eggs are allowed to develop into small groups of cells (4–8 cells). These are embryos.
5. Typically, three of these embryos are then transferred into the uterus via the vagina and cervix.

IVF: Social and Ethical Issues

- Some people object to IVF on religious grounds. Is it right to interfere with a natural process in such an unnatural way?
- What should happen to 'spare' embryos? Should they be destroyed, used for scientific research or be made available to other women?
- Multiple embryos in the uterus increase the risk of miscarriage.
- It is an expensive procedure: between £5000 and £6000 for each attempt.
- Older women who have stopped having periods (post-menopause) can, theoretically, have a baby, meaning some mothers could be in their 70s with a teenage child.

Electrical and Chemical Signals

Diabetes

The body needs controlled quantities of **glucose** for respiration. Glucose is transported in solution by the blood plasma. **Diabetes** is a disease that is caused by the **pancreas** not producing and releasing enough **insulin**. This can lead to a person's blood sugar level rising, resulting in a coma and eventually death.

Control of Blood Glucose

Different parts of the body work together to monitor and control blood glucose levels.

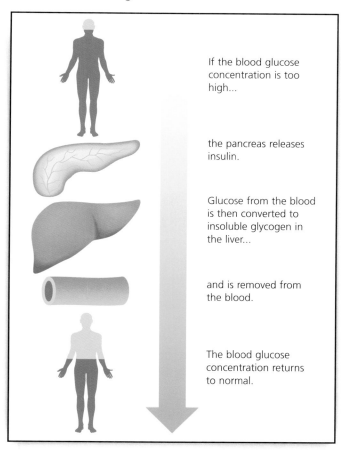

If the blood glucose concentration is too high...

the pancreas releases insulin.

Glucose from the blood is then converted to insoluble glycogen in the liver...

and is removed from the blood.

The blood glucose concentration returns to normal.

Treatment

People who have diabetes can control their blood sugar level by injecting insulin. Before injecting insulin, a person with diabetes will test the amount of sugar in their blood. If they have had food containing a lot of sugar then a bigger dose of insulin is required to reduce their blood sugar level. If they are going to be very active and use up a lot of sugar then a smaller dose of insulin is required prior to them exercising.

Injecting insulin is not the only way of treating diabetes. In some cases diabetes can be controlled by diet (reducing the intake of carbohydrates).

Recently scientists have developed an 'artificial pancreas', which automatically measures blood glucose concentrations and then releases just the right amount of insulin when it is needed. Other scientists have been experimenting with transplanting the insulin-producing cells.

Producing Human Insulin Using Genetically Modified Bacteria

Human insulin can be produced by **genetic engineering**. The gene for insulin production is cut out of human DNA and inserted into a ring of bacterial DNA.

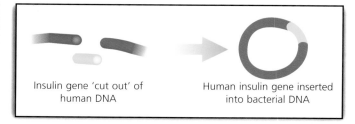

Insulin gene 'cut out' of human DNA

Human insulin gene inserted into bacterial DNA

This bacterial DNA with the new insulin gene is then allowed to reproduce. Eventually there are millions of them, each programmed to produce insulin.

This method of producing insulin is a great breakthrough for diabetics. Not only can the insulin be made more cheaply, but it can be made in large quantities.

Prior to this, bovine (cow) insulin was used. Bovine insulin was not 100% effective and there could be side effects. The situation was worsened with the discovery that BSE could be passed on to humans.

In spite of some opposition to genetic modification of organisms, this is an example where only good has come of it.

Electrical and Chemical Signals

Glossary

Bacteria (singular: bacterium) – a single-celled microorganism that has no nucleus

Brain – part of the central nervous system, it has four main functions: stores information (memory); receives sensory impulses from sense organs; sends out motor impulses to motor organs (muscles and glands); coordinates the actions of the body

Central nervous system (CNS) – consists of the brain and the spinal cord

Contraception – birth control, e.g. the 'pill', the condom. No method is 100% effective

Diabetes – medical condition; the pancreas fails to control blood sugar levels by not producing (enough) insulin

Electrical impulse – electrical message which is passed along neurones when the nervous system communicates with parts of the body

Genetically modified (GM) – an organism which has had DNA (normally a gene) transferred to it from another organism

Glucose – a carbohydrate, sometimes referred to as a simple sugar

Hormone – a chemical (often a protein) produced by an endocrine gland. Hormones are transported in solution in the plasma to their target organ / cell

Infertility – an inability to reproduce

Insulin – hormone produced by the pancreas which controls blood sugar levels in the body

In-vitro fertilisation (IVF) – a technique used to fertilise an ovum (egg) in artificial conditions outside the female's body

Iris reflex – automatic opening and closing of the pupil in response to light conditions

Menstrual cycle – hormonally controlled changes that take place in a woman's reproductive system and result in the monthly replacement of the lining of the uterus

Muscle – an organ made of cells which can change length and therefore produce movement

Oestrogen – a hormone produced by the ovaries: it brings on the development of secondary sexual characteristics in girls and causes the lining of the uterus to thicken during the early part of the menstrual cycle

Pancreas – an organ in the abdomen which produces enzymes to digest food and produces the hormone insulin

Pregnancy – when a fertilised egg develops into an embryo inside a female's body

Progesterone – hormone produced by the ovaries after an egg is released. It preserves and maintains the uterus wall during pregnancy

Reaction time – how quickly it takes you to respond to a stimulus

Receptor – a sense organ that receives information from its surroundings (the environment)

Reflex – an automatic response to a stimulus, over which we have no control. (Reflex actions often protect the body in some way)

Sense organs – the eyes (sight), ears (hearing and balance), taste buds on the tongue (taste), special chemical receptors in the nose (smell) and receptors in the skin (touch)

Stimulus – a change in the surrounding environment which can be detected by a sense organ and which can lead to a response

Target organ – an organ where a specific hormone will have an effect

Voluntary – an action over which we have conscious control

(HT) **Epilepsy** – medical condition caused by the spontaneous and uncoordinated discharge of (electrical) impulses in the brain

Grand mal – a form of epilepsy

Parkinson's disease – a disease of the brain which results in the gradual and progressive inability to move. A common symptom is uncontrollable shaking of the hands

Stroke – caused when part of the brain is starved of oxygen: the brain will stop working properly

Tumour – a swelling which grows as the result of uncontrolled cell divisions (mitosis). May be cancerous

Use, Misuse and Abuse

Solvents, Alcohol and Tobacco

Solvents, alcohol and tobacco can have major physical and mental effects on the human body.

Substance	Effects
Solvents give off different kinds of vapours.	**Physical Effect** (when inhaled) • Can cause permanent damage to the lungs, liver, brain and kidneys. **Mental Effects** • Slow down reaction times by affecting neurones. • Cause hallucinations. • Change behaviour and personality.
Alcohol contains the chemical ethanol.	**Physical Effects** Long-term use can lead to brain damage and liver damage (cirrhosis), because the liver removes alcohol from the body. Excess use can lead to unconsciousness, coma and death. **Mental Effects** • Slows down reaction times by affecting neurones. • Can cause depression. • Can lead to loss of inhibitions and self-control.
Tobacco contains tar and nicotine, and produces carbon monoxide when smoked.	**Physical Effects** Carbon monoxide in smoke is absorbed by haemoglobin in red blood cells more easily than oxygen. Long term use can lead to… • **emphysema:** alveoli become damaged due to excessive coughing • cilia stop 'beating' which causes mucus to build up • bronchitis and other chest infections • damage to the circulatory system: damaged blood vessels which can lead to heart attacks, strokes, arterial and heart disease and even amputations of legs • tar can cause **cancer** • nicotine narrows blood vessels, and increases heart rate and blood pressure. **Mental Effect** • Nicotine is addictive.

Cancer

The tar in cigarette smoke contains **carcinogens** (chemicals that cause cancer). These can cause cells to mutate and divide uncontrollably, which can form tumours. The tar can cause cancer of the lungs, throat, mouth and stomach.

Emphysema

The walls of the alveoli in the lungs break down, reducing the surface area for gaseous exchange. This results in the sufferer having to breathe more deeply in order to compensate for the reduced surface area. This forced breathing in and out results in the chest becoming barrel-shaped.

Use, Misuse and Abuse

How Drugs Can Affect You

Drugs are chemicals which alter the way the body works. Some drugs are obtained from living things (often plants) whilst others are synthetic (man-made). Many drugs are **medicines** used to cure illnesses or ease symptoms. Examples are painkillers and antibiotics (which destroy bacteria).

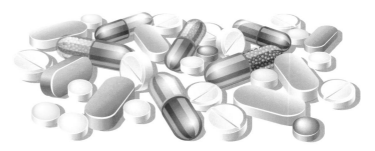

Drug	Effect on nerve transmission and reaction time	Effect on activities such as driving	Abnormal behaviour caused
Caffeine and other stimulants	They speed up the transmission of a message across a synapse (see p.20).	Reactions to things going on around you could become faster.	They can keep you awake leading to physical exhaustion, and can make you highly strung.
Barbiturates and other sedatives	They slow down the transmission of a message across a synapse.	They can make you drowsy so you must not drive or do any other activity that requires full concentration.	They are highly addictive. They can affect you by making you irritable, aggressive, confused and easily upset.
Paracetamol and other painkillers	They prevent the transmission of a message across a synapse.	They can make you drowsy and / or give you blurred vision so you must not drive or do any other activity that requires full concentration.	Side effects include feeling dizzy, or feeling itchy all over.

Paracetamol

Paracetamol is a commonly-used **painkiller** and anti-inflammatory, which also helps to lower body temperature. However, great care must be taken not to exceed the recommended dosage as overdosing can lead to liver failure or death.

Misuse of Drugs

Misuse of drugs can cause both physical and mental problems. Sometimes these are short term. Often the effects last for years.

Sharing unsterilised needles when injecting illegal drugs can lead to an increased risk of spreading viral infections such as hepatitis and HIV.

Cannabinoids and Opiates

Cannabis comes from cannabis plants. **Opiates** are drugs that come from poppy plants.

Both cannabis and opiates are able to relieve pain, especially in the terminally sick. However, they are both **addictive** and are classed as illegal drugs.

Over the years, it has been debated whether they should be used to help patients in pain.

There has been a lot of scientific research into how effective cannabis is in controlling pain. Many doctors and scientists believe there is enough evidence to support the use of cannabis in strictly controlled circumstances. Others feel we still need to do more research into the benefits and the long-term effects.

Use, Misuse and Abuse

Pathogens and Disease

A **pathogen** is a microorganism that causes a disease. There are three main types: bacteria, viruses and fungi.

Bacteria e.g. tuberculosis (TB), conjuctivitis. *Treated by antibiotics.*	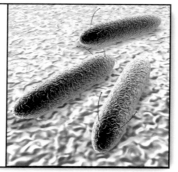
Fungi e.g. athlete's foot, ringworm. *Treated by anti-fungal medicine and antibiotics.*	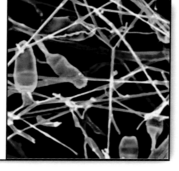
Viruses e.g. Flu, chicken pox, HIV. *Very difficult to treat.*	

Disease transmitted through coughing / sneezing

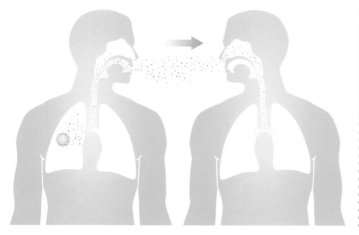

Transmission of Microorganisms

Pathogens (germs) can be transmitted (passed) from one person to another in two main ways:

1 Direct Contact

Some illnesses / diseases are spread by…
- **horizontal transmission**, e.g. touching an ill person.
- **vehicle transmission**, e.g. touching an ill person's things.

Some diseases can be spread directly from mother to foetus. In such cases, the disease will pass across the placenta from the mother's blood to the unborn baby's blood, e.g. HIV. This is an example of **vertical transmission**.

Very few diseases are spread by direct contact.

2 Indirect Contact

Many illnesses / diseases are spread through coughing or sneezing. An infected person's germs are then in the air. Other people may then breathe the germs in and the illness is passed on.

Some diseases are transmitted by a third party: another organism spreads the illness / disease. For example, if someone who has malaria is bitten by a mosquito, the mosquito sucks up a drop of blood. It then flies off and bites another, healthy, person. It transfers some of the ill person's blood to the healthy person. The healthy person then develops malaria because the mosquito has passed the illness on. The mosquito is a **vector** of malaria. Malaria is, therefore, a **vector-borne** disease.

Use, Misuse and Abuse

Keeping Microorganisms Out

The human body has three lines of defence against invading microorganisms:

1. physical and chemical barriers
2. non-specific defences: white blood cells and inflammatory response
3. specific defence: white blood cells and the **immune system**.

Physical and Chemical Barriers

Nasal Hairs

Nasal hairs act like a net, trapping dust and other particles in the air, and preventing them from being breathed into the lungs.

Lysozyme (found in tears)

When bacteria land on the wet surface of the eye they are killed by **lysozyme**. Lysozyme is an enzyme that digests the cell walls of the bacteria.

The Skin

The skin acts as a physical barrier and, as far as possible, prevents...

- entry of disease-causing microorganisms (bacteria and viruses)
- puncture due to injury, friction or continued flexing
- drying out and cracking – the **epidermis** is waterproof and kept supple by oil from the **sebaceous glands**.

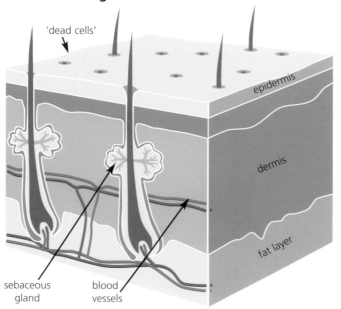

Cilia in the Airways

Specialised cells line the airways of the **respiratory system**. Some produce sticky mucus while others have tiny hairs called **cilia**. The cilia beat and push the mucus upwards towards the mouth. The mucus traps dust and microorganisms which get pushed out of the lungs and are eventually swallowed.

A breathing tube in the lungs

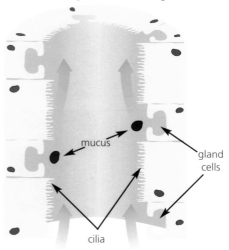

Blood Clotting

Platelets are tiny particles found in blood plasma. They are not cells and they do not have a nucleus. They are very important in helping the blood to clot when a blood vessel has been damaged at a cut.

1. When the skin is cut the platelets in the blood are exposed to air and release an enzyme.

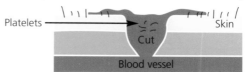

2. The enzyme converts a soluble protein into insoluble fibres of protein called fibrin.

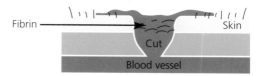

3. The fibrin forms a mesh that traps red blood cells and a clot forms. This hardens to form a scab.

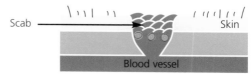

Non-specific Defences

Inflammatory Response

At the site of infection, the blood vessels become enlarged, increasing blood flow to the area and making the skin look red and hot. The capillaries in the skin become more permeable which means that fluids leak out of the blood vessels into the tissues. This causes swelling, or **inflammation**.

White Blood Cells

Where the inflammation has occurred, white blood cells are able to change shape and move out of the blood through the capillary walls into the surrounding tissues and the site of the infection. This type of white blood cell is called a **phagocyte**. Phagocytes ingest the microorganisms and eventually die, forming pus.

Specific Defence

White Blood Cells and the Immune System

White blood cells recognise the microorganisms as **antigens** (foreign bodies) and produce **antibodies** to destroy them (often by making them clump together). We feel ill because it takes time for the white blood cells to produce antibodies to kill the microorganisms.

The production of antibodies is much faster if a person has already had the infectious disease. The white blood cells 'remember' the antigen and, in the future, can produce antibodies more rapidly, providing the person with **natural immunity**. This type of white blood cell is called a **lymphocyte**.

White blood cells also produce anti-toxins which neutralise harmful toxins produced by microorganisms.

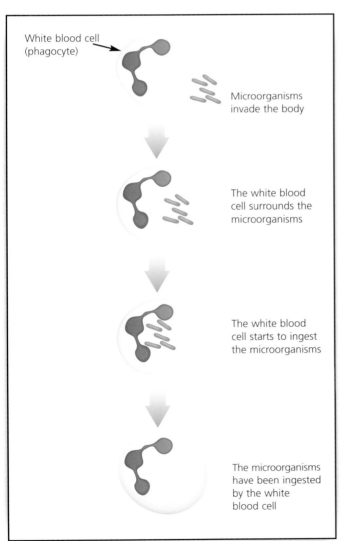

White blood cell (phagocyte)

Microorganisms invade the body

The white blood cell surrounds the microorganisms

The white blood cell starts to ingest the microorganisms

The microorganisms have been ingested by the white blood cell

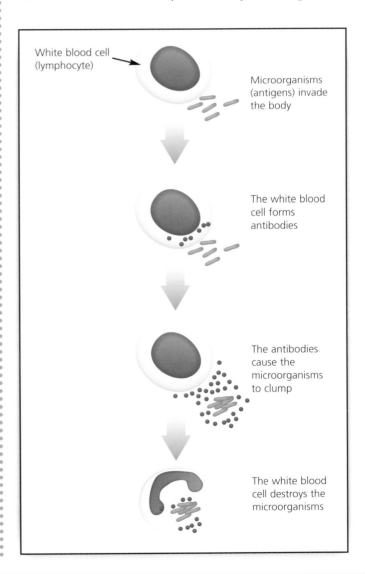

White blood cell (lymphocyte)

Microorganisms (antigens) invade the body

The white blood cell forms antibodies

The antibodies cause the microorganisms to clump

The white blood cell destroys the microorganisms

Use, Misuse and Abuse

Tuberculosis (TB)

TB is a disease caused by the bacterium *Mycobacterium tuberculosis*. Any part of the body can be affected, but it usually infects the lungs. An infected person will spread the disease when they cough and sneeze. The tiny droplets they produce contain the bacteria. If a healthy person breathes in the droplets they are also likely to become infected.

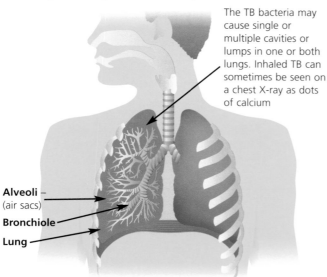

The TB bacteria may cause single or multiple cavities or lumps in one or both lungs. Inhaled TB can sometimes be seen on a chest X-ray as dots of calcium

Alveoli – (air sacs)

Bronchiole

Lung

Research and Development of New Medicines

New drugs and medicines have to be thoroughly tested and trialled before they can be prescribed by doctors. Trialling drugs has three stages:

Is it toxic?	Laboratory tests establish whether the drug is toxic. These tests are often carried out on laboratory animals, like rats.
Is it safe for humans?	Human volunteers trial the drug to establish whether there are any side effects for humans.
Does it work?	People with the illness that the medicine or drug is meant to cure are tested.

These three stages can take years to complete and cost hundreds of thousand of pounds.

Tuberculosis in Britain

In Britain TB tends to be localised in inner cities: London recorded 41% of all cases in 2001 in England, Wales and Northern Ireland. The graph below shows the number of people who became ill with TB in Britain since 1913. Numbers of cases fell dramatically up to 1940, then fell gradually between 1950 and 1990. There has since been a slight increase in cases.

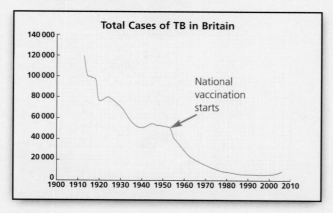

Total Cases of TB in Britain

National vaccination starts

Prevention and Control of Tuberculosis

Prevention (BCG vaccine) – Distributed for the first time in 1953, the BCG vaccine was given to school children around the age of 13. However, because of the costs involved in immunising all pupils, there was a change of policy in 2005 and it was decided to only give the jab to people who were 'at risk'.

Control (drug therapy (antibiotics)) – 'Normal' antibiotics will not kill TB bacteria. A combination of three or four specific anti-TB antibiotics have to be taken for six months. Some people are infected with 'multi-drug-resistant TB' and must take antibiotics for up to 24 months.

Use, Misuse and Abuse

Glossary

Addiction – when a person is dependant on something: a drug. Addiction may be psychological or chemical. Without the drug a person will suffer withdrawal symptoms such as pain, cramp or hallucinations

Alcohol – fermented liquid that has a sedative effect

Antibodies – proteins which are made by white blood cells to destroy microorganisms (antigens) that invade the body

Antigens – foreign bodies which enter the body

Bacteria (singular: bacterium) – a single-celled microorganism that has no nucleus

Barbiturate – a type of sedative

Barrier – a surface that prevents things from passing through

Caffeine – a type of stimulant

Cannabis – an illegal drug obtained from the cannabis plant. It is a hallucinogen

Cilia – small hair-like structures that are found on the surface of some cells, e.g. cells that line the trachea

Circulatory system – consists of the blood, blood vessels (arteries, capillaries and veins) and the heart (a 'pump')

Disease – an illness that is caused by a pathogen

Drug – a chemical substance that alters the way the body works or responds

Foreign body – something in the body that should not be there, e.g. a microorganism, a bit of glass or a wood splinter

Gaseous exchange – the exchange of oxygen and carbon dioxide for respiration. Gaseous exchange happens in the lungs

Immune system – the body's mechanism for defending itself against disease

Infection – occurs when the body is invaded by microorganisms

Inflammation – when part of the skin or body becomes swollen, hot, red and / or painful. It is often the result of infection or injury

Lysozyme – an enzyme that breaks down bacterial cell walls. It is found in tears

Microorganism – an organism that can only be seen with a microscope, e.g. bacteria

Neurone – a cell that carries nerve impulses

Opiate – a drug obtained from opium

Organism – any living thing (i.e. anything that performs the seven features of living things: movement, nutrition, respiration, excretion, growth, reproduction and response)

Overdose – an excessive (usually dangerous) dose of a drug

Pain-relief – stops the transmission of a message across a synapse, therefore relieving pain

Paracetamol – a pain-relief medicine: it prevents the transmission of a message across a synapse

Pathogen – a microorganism that causes a disease

Reaction time – how quickly it takes a person to respond to a stimulus

Sedative – a chemical that slows down the transmission of a message across a synapse

Solvent – a substance that can dissolve other substances. Usually volatile and flammable, solvents can be deliberately inhaled (solvent abuse)

Stimulant – a chemical that speeds up the transmission of a message across a synapse

Tobacco – obtained from the dried leaves of the tobacco plant. It contains nicotine which is highly addictive

Transmission – the transfer of a disease from one individual to another

Tuberculosis – a bacterial infection which develops tubercles (lumps) in the internal organs, often the lungs

Vector-borne – a disease-causing microorganism which is transmitted by another organism (the vector)

Viral infection – an infection caused by a virus

White blood cell – part of the body's immune system: they either engulf bacteria (phagocytes) or produce antibodies (lymphocytes)

Patterns in Properties

The Atom

Atoms are the basic particles from which all matter is made up. All chemical **elements** are made up of atoms.

Atoms have a small nucleus consisting of **protons** and **neutrons**. The nucleus is surrounded by **electrons**. These particles have different relative masses and charges:

Atomic Particle	Relative Mass	Relative Charge
Proton	1	+1 (positive)
Neutron	1	0
Electron	0 (nearly)	-1 (negative)

An atom has the same number of protons as electrons, so the atom as a whole has no electrical charge.

All the atoms of a particular element have the same number of protons in their nuclei. All the atoms of a particular element have the same number of electrons orbiting the nucleus.

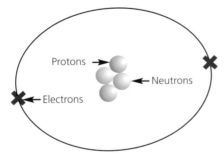

A Simple Example: Helium Atom

The **mass number** of an element is the total number of protons and neutrons in the atom.

The **atomic number** of an element is the number of protons (or electrons) in one atom.

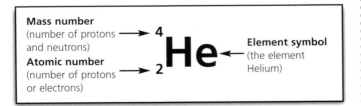

Mass number (number of protons and neutrons) → 4
Atomic number (number of protons or electrons) → 2
$_2^4\text{He}$
Element symbol (the element Helium)

Molecules and Compounds

A **molecule** is formed when two or more atoms are joined together. Molecules can be formed from the atoms of one type of element, or two or more types of element. **Diatomic molecules** consist of two atoms of the same element e.g. O_2, H_2.

A **compound** is formed from two or more elements which have been joined together to form molecules in a chemical reaction. The compound's properties will be different to the properties of the individual elements it is made up from. Consider what happens when iron and sulphur are heated:

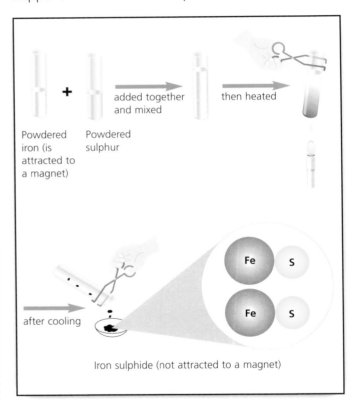

Powdered iron (is attracted to a magnet)   Powdered sulphur   added together and mixed   then heated

after cooling

Fe   S
Fe   S

Iron sulphide (not attracted to a magnet)

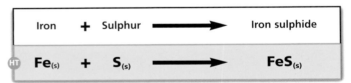

| Iron | + | Sulphur | → | Iron sulphide |

HT $Fe_{(s)}$ + $S_{(s)}$ → $FeS_{(s)}$

The compound iron sulphide contains lots of molecules that consist of one iron atom joined to one sulphur atom.

Once formed, compounds can only be split into simpler substances (elements) through chemical reactions.

Chemical Reactions

A **chemical reaction** involves two or more **reactants** combining together to make new substances known as **products**. A product may be an element or a compound.

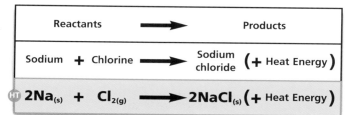

Chemical reactions happen at different rates (e.g. within seconds or even days) and are usually accompanied by a temperature change, which can be...

- **exothermic** – thermal (heat) energy is released
- **endothermic** – thermal energy is taken in.

HT Balancing Equations

All chemical reactions follow the same simple rule: the mass of the reactants is equal to the mass of the products.

This means there must be the same number of atoms on both sides of the equation.

Number of atoms in reactants = Number of atoms in products

Writing Balanced Equations

1. Write down the word equation for the reaction.
2. Write down the correct formula for each of the reactants and the products.
3. Check that there are the same numbers of each atom on both sides of the equation.

If the equation is already balanced leave it. If the equation needs balancing…

1. Write a number in front of one or more of the formulae. This increases the number of all of the atoms in the formula.
2. Don't forget the state symbols: (s) = solid, (l) = liquid, (g) = gas and (aq) = dissolved in water (aqueous solution).

Example

Balance the reaction between sodium and water.

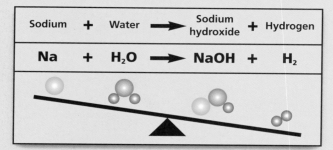

There are more hydrogen atoms on the products side than on the reactants side so, balance hydrogen by doubling the amount of water and sodium hydroxide:

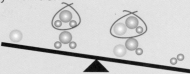

The amount of oxygen and hydrogen on both sides is equal. However, the amount of sodium is now unequal.

Double the sodium on the reactant side to match the amount of sodium on the products side:

This should now give you a balanced equation.

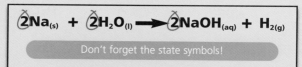

Don't forget the state symbols!

Patterns in Properties

The Periodic Table

Elements are the building blocks of all materials. The 100 or so elements are arranged in the **periodic table**, in order of increasing atomic number. The elements are arranged in rows (**periods**) so that elements with similar properties are in the same column (**group**). This forms the basis of the periodic table (a detailed version is on page 104).

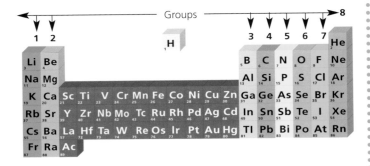

- More than three quarters of the elements are metals.
- Metals are found mainly in Groups 1 and 2 and in the central block.
- Group 1 elements are known as the **alkali metals**.
- Group 7 elements are known as the **halogens**.
- Group 8 elements are known as the **noble gases**.
- The central block of elements between Group 2 and Group 3 is the **transition metals**.

Trends in the Periodic Table

- The elements in a particular group have similar chemical properties since they have the same number of electrons in their outermost shell.
- The size and mass of the elements get bigger as we go from left to right across a period (row).
- Elements in Group 1 (which all have 1 electron in their outermost shell) become more reactive as we go down the group.
- Elements in Group 7 (which all have 7 electrons in their outermost shell) become less reactive as we go down the group.

The periodic table can be used to predict the properties of new and undiscovered elements.

The History of the Periodic Table

Before the modern periodic table was developed, a number of attempts were made to arrange the elements:

1817: Johann Dobereiner, a German scientist, developed the 'law of triads'. Each triad consisted of three elements whose reactions and appearances were similar.

1864: John Newlands, an English scientist, proposed the 'octaves principal'.
- All known elements were arranged in order of relative atomic mass.
- The elements were written down in rows of 7.
- He found that every eighth element had similar properties. However, this did not work for the heavier elements.

1869: Russian chemist **Dimitri Mendeleev** developed the modern periodic table.
- The elements were again arranged in order of relative atomic mass.
- The table included all the known elements and left gaps for those not yet discovered.
- Each element was put into a group (column) where it fitted best.
- Elements that did not fit were put into a spare column.
- Mendeleev was able to work out the atomic mass and properties of undiscovered elements.

1913: British chemist **Henry Moseley** proposed the use of **atomic number** to arrange the elements, rather than atomic mass, leading to the modern periodic table.

The Alkali Metals

The **alkali metals** occupy the first vertical group (Group 1) at the left-hand side of the periodic table. Lithium, sodium and potassium are typical members of this group.

More reactive with increasing atomic number. Lower melting and boiling points

Group 1	
7	**Li** Lithium
3	
23	**Na** Sodium
11	
39	**K** Potassium
19	
85	**Rb** Rubidium
37	

Properties of the Alkali Metals

- They are soft and have low melting points (e.g. potassium has a melting point of 63°C).
- They become increasingly exothermic in their reactions with water.
- Their high degree of reactivity means they must be stored under oil.
- The further down Group 1 the metal is, the greater its reactivity.
- The further down Group 1 the metal is, the further away the lone outer electron is from the nucleus.
- Francium is the most reactive alkali metal: it is unstable and is a radioactive element.
- They react vigorously with water to form hydroxides which are alkaline (higher than 7 on the pH scale), and hydrogen gas.

We can perform a simple test for hydrogen gas: Hydrogen collected in the inverted test tube makes a squeaky pop when lit.

Pop!

Test tube of hydrogen

Lighted splint

Reactions of the Alkali Metals

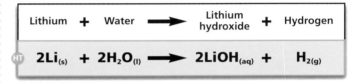

Li

Lithium	+	Water	→	Lithium hydroxide	+	Hydrogen

HT $2Li_{(s)} + 2H_2O_{(l)} \longrightarrow 2LiOH_{(aq)} + H_{2(g)}$

K

Potassium	+	Water	→	Potassium hydroxide	+	Hydrogen

HT $2K_{(s)} + 2H_2O_{(l)} \longrightarrow 2KOH_{(aq)} + H_{2(g)}$

Caesium	+	Water	→	Caesium hydroxide	+	Hydrogen

HT $2Cs_{(s)} + 2H_2O_{(l)} \longrightarrow 2CsOH_{(aq)} + H_{2(g)}$

Patterns in Properties

The Transition Metals

The **transition metals** include all the elements between Group 2 and Group 3 in the periodic table. Iron and copper are well-known examples of transition elements and they are located in the first (upper) row of the transition metals block.

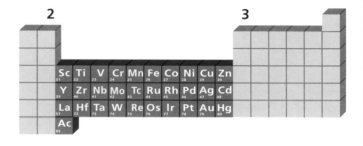

Properties of the Transition Metals

- Transition metals are hard and dense and have high melting points.
- They are good conductors of heat and electricity.
- They are not very reactive: silver and gold can be found unreacted in the ground.
- Transition metal compounds are often coloured (e.g. copper sulphate crystals are blue).

Reactions of the Transition Metals

Many transition metals will form solids in solution when they are reacted with dilute sodium hydroxide. This **precipitation reaction** is used to help identify an unknown metal within a compound. For example...

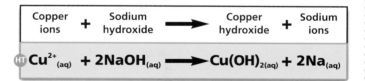

| Copper ions | + | Sodium hydroxide | → | Copper hydroxide | + | Sodium ions |

$$Cu^{2+}_{(aq)} + 2NaOH_{(aq)} \longrightarrow Cu(OH)_{2(aq)} + 2Na_{(aq)}$$

Colour of Precipitate	Metal ions present		Solid dissolves in ammonia solution
Pale blue	Copper	Cu^{2+}	Yes
Green	Iron	Fe^{2+}	No
Red-brown	Iron	Fe^{3+}	No
White	Zinc	Zn^{2+}	Yes

Uses of the Transition Metals

The transition metals are used to make objects such as wires, coins, medicine, girders, ornaments, jewellery etc. The transition metals and their compounds are also used to make alloys (mixtures of metals which are stronger than one metal alone) and as **catalysts**. For example, in the **Haber process**, an iron catalyst is used to speed up the reaction between nitrogen and hydrogen to produce ammonia gas:

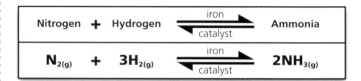

The Noble Gases

The **noble gases** are located in a vertical group at the right-hand side of the periodic table. This is called Group 8 or Group 0 (depending on which book or chart you look at). The noble gases do not have a smell and cannot be seen, however, they glow with a particular colour when electricity passes through them.

All the elements in Group 8 are **chemically inert**, i.e. unreactive, compared with elements in other groups of the periodic table.

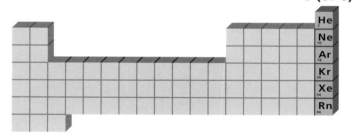

Uses of the Noble Gases

- Helium is used in airships and weather balloons because it is much less dense than air and is non-flammable.
- Argon is used in light bulbs because it is unreactive and provides an inert atmosphere.
- Argon, krypton and neon are all used in fluorescent lights and discharge tubes.

Patterns in Properties

The Halogens

The **halogens** are found in Group 7 of the periodic table. There are five non-metals in Group 7; the top four are the ones you need to remember. They all vary in colour. Their melting and boiling points determine their physical state at room temperature. The halogens all exist as diatomic molecules.

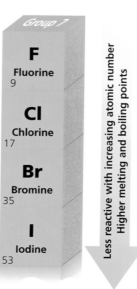

Group 7

F
Fluorine
9

Cl
Chlorine
17

Br
Bromine
35

I
Iodine
53

Less reactive with increasing atomic number
Higher melting and boiling points

Halogen	Fluorine	Chlorine	Bromine	Iodine
Boiling Point (°C)	-188°C	-34°C	59°C (melting point -7°C)	184°C (melting point 114°C)
Colour and physical state at room temperature	Pale yellow vapour	Pale green vapour	Red-brown liquid	Grey solid

Displacement Reactions

The halogens' atomic numbers increase as we go down the group and they become less reactive. This can be shown by the **displacement reactions** of halogens with solutions of other **halides**. In summary...

- chlorine is the most reactive
- bromine and iodine are the least reactive

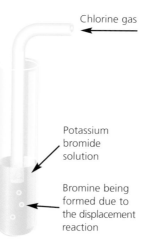

Chlorine gas

Potassium bromide solution

Bromine being formed due to the displacement reaction

	Potassium Chloride	Potassium Bromide	Potassium Iodide
Chlorine Cl₂	✕	Potassium chloride	Potassium chloride
Bromine Br₂	No reaction	✕	Potassium bromide
Iodine I₂	No reaction	No reaction	✕

Uses of the Halogens

Chlorine is used in water purification, e.g. swimming pools and domestic water supplies, as it kills bacteria. It is also used for bleaching paper, wood and cloth. Iodine solution is used as an antiseptic.

Reactions of Halogens and Iron

Iron, in the form of iron wool, is heated strongly and **chlorine** gas is passed over it in a fume cupboard. The iron wool will glow brightly as the following reaction takes place:

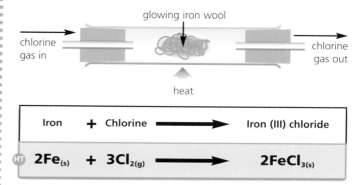

glowing iron wool

chlorine gas in

chlorine gas out

heat

| Iron | + | Chlorine | → | Iron (III) chloride |

(HT) $2Fe_{(s)} + 3Cl_{2(g)} \longrightarrow 2FeCl_{3(s)}$

When the iron wool is heated strongly with **bromine**, the iron wool does not glow as brightly but the reaction is the same:

bromine liquid

iron wool

heat

| Iron | + | Bromine | → | Iron (III) bromide |

(HT) $2Fe_{(s)} + 3Br_{2(g)} \longrightarrow 2FeBr_{3(s)}$

Iodine will react the same way with the iron wool but the iron wool will glow the least brightly:

iodine crystals

iron wool

heat

| Iron | + | Iodine | → | Iron (III) iodide |

(HT) $2Fe_{(s)} + 3I_{2(g)} \longrightarrow 2FeI_{3(s)}$

Patterns in Properties

Metal Compounds and Flame Tests

A **metal compound** is formed when a metal reacts with a non-metal or a non-metal compound. Simple tests, such as **flame tests**, can be used to identify the metal within a compound. When metal ions are heated in a flame they will burn with a signature colour.

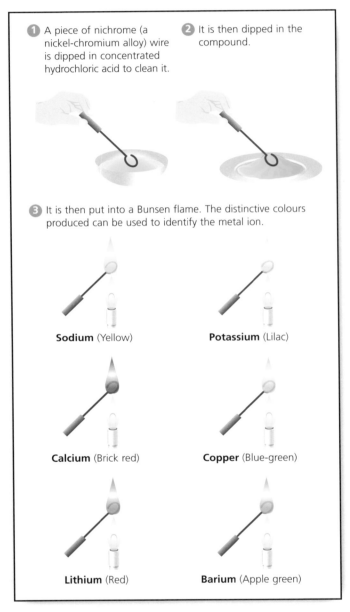

① A piece of nichrome (a nickel-chromium alloy) wire is dipped in concentrated hydrochloric acid to clean it.

② It is then dipped in the compound.

③ It is then put into a Bunsen flame. The distinctive colours produced can be used to identify the metal ion.

Sodium (Yellow)

Potassium (Lilac)

Calcium (Brick red)

Copper (Blue-green)

Lithium (Red)

Barium (Apple green)

By understanding how different chemicals behave and the tests used to identify them, scientists can use these analytical techniques to identify unknown substances. This can be very useful, for example, in forensic science (crime investigations). You might be asked to identify substances from their properties in the exam, so make sure you know them.

Naming Metal Compounds

There are a few general and simple rules to remember when naming metal compounds:

- The metal's name is always written first.
- Change the ending of the name of the non-metal to –ide, but only when there is one non-metal present.
- If there are two non-metals present and one of them is oxygen, then end the name in –ate.

For example...

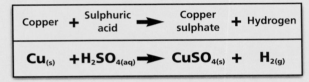

| Copper | + | Sulphuric acid | → | Copper sulphate | + | Hydrogen |

$$Cu_{(s)} + H_2SO_{4(aq)} \rightarrow CuSO_{4(s)} + H_{2(g)}$$

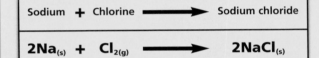

| Sodium | + | Chlorine | → | Sodium chloride |

$$2Na_{(s)} + Cl_{2(g)} \rightarrow 2NaCl_{(s)}$$

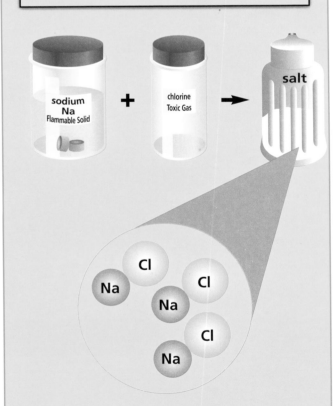

sodium
Na
Flammable Solid

chlorine
Toxic Gas

salt

So, one atom of sodium plus one atom of chlorine produces sodium chloride.

Patterns in Properties

Glossary

Alkali metal – an element found in Group 1 of the periodic table. Atoms of these elements all contain a single electron in their outer energy level

Analytical – a variety of methods used to identify the chemical components of substances

Atomic number – the number of protons in the nucleus of an atom or the number of electrons orbiting the nucleus

Atom – the smallest particle of a chemical element that shows the properties of the element

Compound – a substance that contains atoms of two or more elements that have been chemically combined

Diatomic molecule – two atoms of the same element held together by a single covalent bond, which cannot occur as single atoms.

Displacement reaction – a chemical reaction in which a more reactive element replaces a less reactive element in the compound

Electron – a negatively charged particle which orbits the nucleus of an atom. It has a negligible mass

Element – a pure substance that is made from just one type of atom. It cannot be split into a simpler chemical

Endothermic – a chemical reaction that takes in energy from the surroundings in the form of heat

Exothermic – a chemical reaction that gives out energy to the surroundings in the form of heat

Flame test – a test to identify a metal in a compound from the colour of flame produced

Formula – a written representation of the elements present in a chemical compound that shows the number of atoms of each element present

Group – a vertical column of the periodic table where elements have similar properties

Halide – the salts produced from the reaction between metals and the halogens

Halogens – non-metals found in Group 7 of the periodic table. Known as the 'salt-formers', they exist as diatomic molecules

Inert – a substance that is chemically unreactive

Molecule – the smallest part of an element or compound that can exist on its own

Neutron – an uncharged particle found in the nucleus of almost all atoms.

Noble gases – unreactive, non-metallic elements found in Group 8 (or 0) of the periodic table

Period – a horizontal row of elements in the periodic table with a variety of properties and the same number of electron shells

Precipitation – when an insoluble solid is formed in a solution as a result of a chemical reaction

Proton – a positively charged particle found in the nucleus of every atom.

Solution – produced when a substance is dissolved in another substance, e.g. water will dissolve salt to make salt water solution

Symbols – abbreviations that are used to identify elements and compounds instead of using their full names

Transition metals – found in the central block of the periodic table. They include many of the metals which are encountered everyday

Making Changes

Metal Ores

Ores are naturally occurring rocks found in the Earth's crust. They contain compounds of metals in sufficient amounts to make it worthwhile extracting them.

Some of these compounds are **metal oxides**, e.g. iron oxide (haematite). The method of extracting a metal from its ore depends on the metal's position in the **reactivity series**.

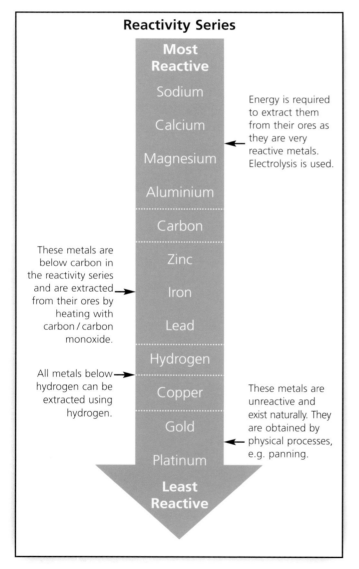

Reactivity Series

Most Reactive

Sodium

Calcium — Energy is required to extract them from their ores as they are very reactive metals. Electrolysis is used.

Magnesium

Aluminium

Carbon

These metals are below carbon in the reactivity series and are extracted from their ores by heating with carbon / carbon monoxide. →

Zinc

Iron

Lead

Hydrogen

All metals below → hydrogen can be extracted using hydrogen.

Copper — These metals are unreactive and exist naturally. They are obtained by physical processes, e.g. panning.

Gold

Platinum

Least Reactive

The most reactive metals form the most stable ores and are therefore most difficult to extract.

The least reactive metals are found uncombined in the Earth's crust and are the easiest to extract from their ores.

When a mixture of iron oxide and aluminium powder is heated, an extremely vigorous reaction takes place. The heat released is great enough to melt the reduced iron.

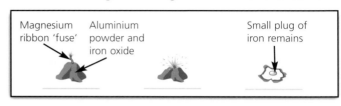

Magnesium ribbon 'fuse'   Aluminium powder and iron oxide   Small plug of iron remains

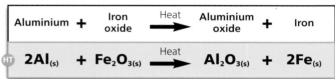

| Aluminium | + | Iron oxide | $\xrightarrow{\text{Heat}}$ | Aluminium oxide | + | Iron |

HT $2Al_{(s)} + Fe_2O_{3(s)} \xrightarrow{\text{Heat}} Al_2O_{3(s)} + 2Fe_{(s)}$

Reduction

Reduction is the loss of oxygen from a compound during a chemical reaction. It is the process through which a metal compound is broken down to give the metal element. For example…

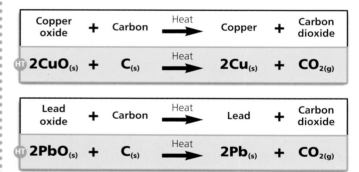

| Copper oxide | + | Carbon | $\xrightarrow{\text{Heat}}$ | Copper | + | Carbon dioxide |

HT $2CuO_{(s)} + C_{(s)} \xrightarrow{\text{Heat}} 2Cu_{(s)} + CO_{2(g)}$

| Lead oxide | + | Carbon | $\xrightarrow{\text{Heat}}$ | Lead | + | Carbon dioxide |

HT $2PbO_{(s)} + C_{(s)} \xrightarrow{\text{Heat}} 2Pb_{(s)} + CO_{2(g)}$

Oxidation

When a metal, a compound or any other element combines with oxygen to make other substances, it is called **oxidation**. Oxidation is the gaining of oxygen by an element or compound. For example, when magnesium is heated with oxygen it is oxidised to produce magnesium oxide.

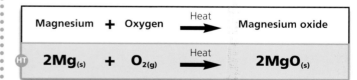

| Magnesium | + | Oxygen | $\xrightarrow{\text{Heat}}$ | Magnesium oxide |

HT $2Mg_{(s)} + O_{2(g)} \xrightarrow{\text{Heat}} 2MgO_{(s)}$

- When copper oxide and lead oxide are heated with carbon, the carbon is oxidised to produce **carbon dioxide**.
- When aluminium is heated with iron oxide, the aluminium is oxidised to produce **aluminium oxide**.

Making Salts

A neutral salt is formed when an acid is reacted with a base. (Some bases are soluble in water and dissolve to produce alkaline solutions.) This type of reaction is called a **neutralisation** reaction. The salts formed in these reactions are soluble salts and they can only be obtained when the water is evaporated off.

Using an Alkaline Hydroxide Base

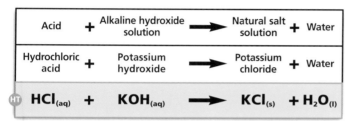

Acid	+	Alkaline hydroxide solution	→	Natural salt solution	+	Water
Hydrochloric acid	+	Potassium hydroxide	→	Potassium chloride	+	Water

$$\text{HCl}_{(aq)} + \text{KOH}_{(aq)} \longrightarrow \text{KCl}_{(s)} + \text{H}_2\text{O}_{(l)}$$

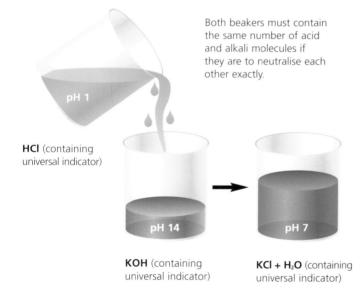

Both beakers must contain the same number of acid and alkali molecules if they are to neutralise each other exactly.

HCl (containing universal indicator)

KOH (containing universal indicator)

KCl + H₂O (containing universal indicator)

Using a Metal Oxide Base

Acid	+	Metal oxide	→	Natural salt solution	+	Water
Sulphuric acid	+	Copper oxide	→	Copper sulphate	+	Water

$$\text{H}_2\text{SO}_{4(aq)} + \text{CuO}_{(s)} \longrightarrow \text{CuSO}_{4(s)} + \text{H}_2\text{O}_{(l)}$$

Using a Metal Carbonate Base

Acid	+	Metal carbonate	→	Natural salt solution	+	Water	+	Carbon dioxide
Sulphuric acid	+	Calcium carbonate	→	Calcium sulphate	+	Water	+	Carbon dioxide

$$\text{H}_2\text{SO}_{4(aq)} + \text{CaCO}_{3(s)} \longrightarrow \text{CaSO}_{4(aq)} + \text{H}_2\text{O}_{(l)} + \text{CO}_{2(g)}$$

The particular salt produced depends on the acid, and the metal in the base used. They all react in the same way but produce different salts. As a rule, sulphuric acid will always produce sulphate salts, and hydrochloric acid will always produce chloride salts.

Some salts formed during neutralisation reactions are insoluble salts; a **precipitate** is formed when two soluble salt solutions are mixed together. For example...

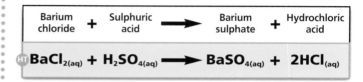

Barium chloride	+	Sulphuric acid	→	Barium sulphate	+	Hydrochloric acid

$$\text{BaCl}_{2(aq)} + \text{H}_2\text{SO}_{4(aq)} \longrightarrow \text{BaSO}_{4(aq)} + 2\text{HCl}_{(aq)}$$

The pure salt can be retrieved by filtering off the acid, washing it with distilled water and drying it in a warm oven.

Uses of Salts

Salts can be used...

- as fertilisers, e.g. ammonium nitrate
- in fireworks, e.g. barium salts produce green colours, strontium salts produce red colours
- for colouring glass, enamels, paints, dyes etc., e.g. copper salts are used for making turquoise glass
- Some salts are added to fuels to improve **combustion** and reduce the pollutants given off.

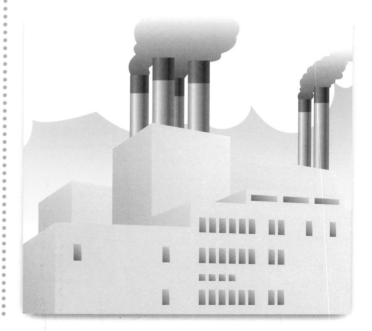

Making Changes

Hazard Labels

Symbols are used to identify any form of chemical hazard.

Toxic

These substances can kill. They can act when you swallow them, breathe them in or absorb them through your skin.
Example: chlorine gas.

Oxidising

These substances provide oxygen, which allows other substances to burn more fiercely.
Example: hydrogen peroxide.

Harmful

These substances are similar to toxic substances but they are less dangerous.
Example: lead oxide.

Highly Flammable

These substances will catch fire easily. They pose a serious fire risk.
Example: hydrogen.

Corrosive

These substances attack other materials and living tissue, including eyes and skin.
Example: concentrated sulphuric acid.

Irritant

These substances are not corrosive but they can cause blistering of the skin.
Example: calcium chloride.

Chemical Substances

Everything around us is made of chemicals. There is no alternative to chemicals, only in how they are used or made. Some chemical substances are **natural** and some are **artificial** (man-made or synthetic).

Using natural chemicals does not necessarily mean that they are better for you. For example…

- henna tattoos, bee / wasp stings, peanuts etc. can all cause allergic reactions
- untreated water can kill
- rotting fruit contains toxins that can make people ill
- all potatoes contain some poison.

Artificial substances are much more reliable because they have been made with a specific composition in a controlled environment. The ability to create or extract chemical substances allows us to eliminate some of nature's impurities and toxic effects.

Chemical	Natural or Artificial?	Effect
Histamine	Natural	Inflammation or anaphylactic shock
Anti-histamine	Artificial	Reduces mild irritation and inflammation caused by histamine
Foxglove flowers	Natural	Poisonous – could kill
Digitalis	Artificial	Extracted from foxglove flowers in the lab and used to treat heart conditions

It is not always possible to determine the difference between man-made and natural substances because the man-made substance has been chemically designed to be the same as the natural substance. Quite often they will both look the same.

Making Changes

Chemical Reactions in cooking

Cooking food is the process of using heat to create edible products through a variety of chemical reactions. Generally, food undergoes three main changes when heated: appearance, flavour and texture.

Different ways of cooking generate different reactions as they all happen at different temperatures. If we use oil to cook with then the combination of heat, oil and the internal make-up of the food will govern how the chemical reaction changes the food.

Meat browns when it is cooked because the rise in temperature triggers a reaction between amino acids and carbohydrates. All foods will brown if they are heated at a temperature of 154°C.

Sodium hydrogen carbonate (baking powder) is used to create baked goods that rise and have a delicate structure, such as biscuits and muffins. The chemical works by releasing an initial set of carbon dioxide bubbles when it is mixed with the wet ingredients. When the mixture is heated, larger bubbles are released creating further lift in the baked product. This can only happen if the mixture is not fully cooked. Once it is cooked the air pockets are fixed in position and the product cannot rise any more.

ⒽⓉ Food Chemicals and Health

Some chemicals that are added to food may result in adverse side effects such as hyperactivity disorders. Scientific research has linked additives (e.g. sweeteners and flavourings) to hyperactivity in children: a recent report suggested that if such additives were taken out of children's food, hyperactivity cases would go down from 17% to 6%. However, this remaining 6% suggests that the chemical may not always be responsible for the occurrence of hyperactivity.

Thermal Decomposition

Thermal decomposition is the breaking down of a substance into simpler substances through heating.

If we heat calcium hydrogen carbonate it will decompose into calcium carbonate, carbon dioxide and water.

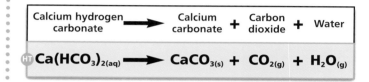

$$\text{ⒽⓉ } Ca(HCO_3)_{2(aq)} \longrightarrow CaCO_{3(s)} + CO_{2(g)} + H_2O_{(g)}$$

If the calcium carbonate is heated, then it too will decompose into calcium oxide and carbon dioxide.

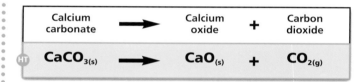

$$\text{ⒽⓉ } CaCO_{3(s)} \longrightarrow CaO_{(s)} + CO_{2(g)}$$

Reactions with Water

When blue copper sulphate crystals are heated, they break down into anhydrous copper sulphate, a white powder. This can be **reversed**. If you add water to the white powder you will get the blue crystals back again. This is a **hydration** reaction.

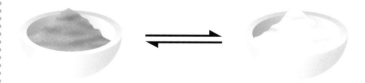

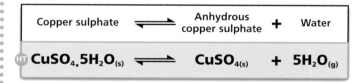

$$\text{ⒽⓉ } CuSO_4.5H_2O_{(s)} \rightleftharpoons CuSO_{4(s)} + 5H_2O_{(g)}$$

We can **dehydrate** sucrose by adding concentrated sulphuric acid to it. This is a **dehydration** reaction.

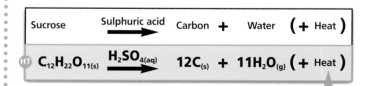

$$\text{ⒽⓉ } C_{12}H_{22}O_{11(s)} \xrightarrow{H_2SO_{4(aq)}} 12C_{(s)} + 11H_2O_{(g)} (+ Heat)$$

This tells us it is an exothermic reaction

Making Changes

Gases from Chemical Reactions

Collecting Gases

There are a number of ways in which gases can be collected when they are produced as a result of a chemical reaction.

Method used to collect gas	Upward delivery of air	Downward delivery of air	Over water	Gas syringe
This method can be used when...	the gas produced is heavier than air.	the gas produced is lighter than air.	the gas is sparingly soluble in water.	you want to measure the volume of gas produced.
Type of apparatus used to collect the gas	Gas jar	Gas jar	Gas jar	Gas Syringe
Examples of gases that can be collected this way	Carbon dioxide, CO_2 Chlorine, Cl_2	Ammonia, NH_3 Hydrogen, H_2	Carbon dioxide, CO_2 Oxygen, O_2 Hydrogen, H_2	Any gas

Testing Gases

There are various ways in which gases can be tested.
The test for the gas is based on its particular properties.

Gas	Ammonia, NH_3	Oxygen, O_2	Hydrogen, H_2	Chlorine, Cl_2	Carbon dioxide, CO_2
Properties	A colourless alkaline gas with a pungent smell.	A colourless gas which helps fuels burn more readily than in air.	A colourless gas. It combines violently with oxygen when ignited.	A green poisonous gas which bleaches dyes.	A colourless, mildly acidic gas that turns limewater milky.
Test for Gas	Turns damp indicator paper blue.	Relights a glowing splint.	Burns with a squeaky pop.	Turns damp indicator paper white.	Turns lime water cloudy or milky.

Making Changes

Common Compounds

Compounds are formed when two or more elements are joined together as a result of a chemical reaction. These compounds can be…

- **natural** substances such as citric acid, ammonia, carbohydrates, sodium chloride, water, carbon dioxide and ethanoic (acetic) acid
- **artificial** (or manufactured) substances such as caustic soda, phosphoric acid and hydrochloric acid.

Compound	Uses	Compound	Uses
Citric acid	• in the production of soft drinks, laxatives and cathartics.	**Ethanoic acid** (also known as **acetic acid**)	• for preserving food • as a condiment • in the production of acetate rayon, plastics, photographic film, paint, solvents and pharmaceuticals.
Ammonia	• in the production of fertilisers, dyes, paints, bleaches and hydrolysing oils and fats.	**Hydrochloric acid**	• in the production of other chemicals. • to process glucose and other foods.
Carbohydrates	• in the production of fats • to make fabrics, plastics and photographic film • in the preparation of animal feed, adhesives and emulsions.	**Phosphoric acid**	• for cleaning and rust-proofing metals • in acidifying jellies and beverages.
Carbon dioxide	• in the production of carbonated drinks • as a raising agent • to make lead-paint pigments and aspirin • in fire extinguishers • in aerosol food cans.	**Sodium chloride** (**table salt**)	• as a seasoning or preservative for foods • in making soap, textile dyes, glass and pottery • in chemical production.
Caustic soda (the common name for **sodium hydroxide**)	• in the manufacture of other chemicals and whenever a strong base is needed • in the production of paper, textiles, soaps and detergents.	**Water** (an important part of living organisms)	• as a powerful industrial cutting tool • as energy production in power stations • as a lubricant.

Making Changes

Glossary

Carbohydrates – chemical compounds of carbon, hydrogen and oxygen, such as sugars and starches

Caustic soda – the common name for sodium hydroxide, a strong alkali used to make chemicals and soaps; very corrosive

Citric acid – a weak acid that can be found in all citrus fruits, which is soluble in water

Combustion – an exothermic reaction between a fuel and a gas (usually oxygen) releasing heat and, in most cases, light

Decomposition – a chemical reaction that breaks down large molecules into smaller molecules or atoms

Dehydration – the removal of water from a substance

Dilute – the process of adding water to a solution to make it weaker / less concentrated

Hydration – the addition of water to a substance

Insoluble salt – a solid that will not dissolve in a liquid, or a solid that is formed in chemical reactions that involve solutions

Neutralisation – reacting a base or alkali with acid to form a salt and water with a pH of 7

Oxidation – the combination of oxygen with elements or compounds, converting them into other substances

Precipitate – an insoluble substance that is formed in chemical reactions which involve solutions

Reduction – the loss of oxygen from a compound, during a chemical reaction

Salt – a substance that is formed as a result of a neutralisation reaction between an acid and a base / alkali

Soluble salt – a salt that will easily dissolve in a liquid, or a salt that is in solution when it is formed

Thermal decomposition – using heat to break down a large molecule into smaller molecules or atoms

The Atmosphere

Since the formation of the Earth 4.6 billion years ago, the atmosphere has changed dramatically.

The timescale, however, is enormous: one billion years is one thousand million (1 000 000 000) years.

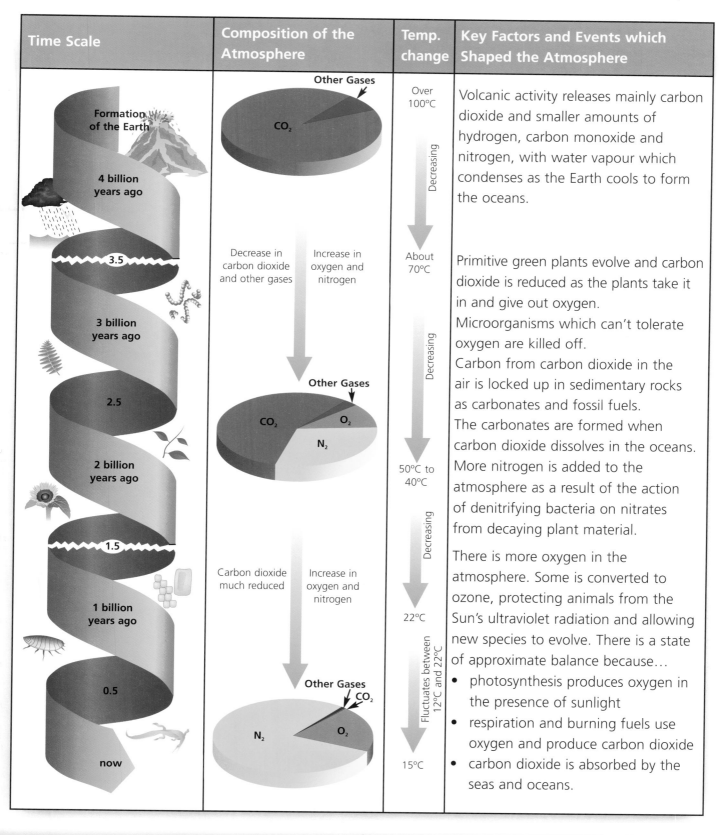

Time Scale	Composition of the Atmosphere	Temp. change	Key Factors and Events which Shaped the Atmosphere
Formation of the Earth 4 billion years ago 3.5	**Other Gases** CO₂	Over 100°C ↓ Decreasing	Volcanic activity releases mainly carbon dioxide and smaller amounts of hydrogen, carbon monoxide and nitrogen, with water vapour which condenses as the Earth cools to form the oceans.
3 billion years ago 2.5 2 billion years ago	Decrease in carbon dioxide and other gases / Increase in oxygen and nitrogen **Other Gases** CO₂ O₂ N₂	About 70°C ↓ Decreasing 50°C to 40°C	Primitive green plants evolve and carbon dioxide is reduced as the plants take it in and give out oxygen. Microorganisms which can't tolerate oxygen are killed off. Carbon from carbon dioxide in the air is locked up in sedimentary rocks as carbonates and fossil fuels. The carbonates are formed when carbon dioxide dissolves in the oceans. More nitrogen is added to the atmosphere as a result of the action of denitrifying bacteria on nitrates from decaying plant material.
1.5 1 billion years ago 0.5 now	Carbon dioxide much reduced / Increase in oxygen and nitrogen **Other Gases** CO₂ N₂ O₂	↓ Decreasing 22°C Fluctuates between 12°C and 22°C 15°C	There is more oxygen in the atmosphere. Some is converted to ozone, protecting animals from the Sun's ultraviolet radiation and allowing new species to evolve. There is a state of approximate balance because… • photosynthesis produces oxygen in the presence of sunlight • respiration and burning fuels use oxygen and produce carbon dioxide • carbon dioxide is absorbed by the seas and oceans.

There's One Earth

Global Warming

Global warming is the accelerated increase in the average temperature of the surface of the Earth due to an increase in the levels of greenhouse gases (e.g. carbon dioxide, methane, sulphur dioxide, nitrogen oxide and carbon monoxide).

In the early 20th century, Svante Arrhenius, a Swedish chemist, predicted that CO_2 levels in the atmosphere would double within 3000 years, resulting in a potential global temperature increase of 5°C brought about by industrialisation.

By the 1960s and 1970s the opposite was thought to be happening: global cooling. By the late 1970s and mid-1980s, **computer-simulated models** were predicting an increase in the Earth's temperature of 4°C and a doubling of the level of CO_2 in the atmosphere within a century. However, there are always uncertainties with computer simulations.

By the late 1980s the theory of global warming was widely accepted. This was a result of scientific evidence and findings which showed that sea ice in the Arctic ocean had thinned by 40% since the 1970s and that the Earth's temperature has risen by 0.5°C in the last century.

Causes of Global Warming

Throughout its history the temperature of the Earth has fluctuated. But in the 20th century, scientists recognised that industrialisation was causing more 'greenhouse gases' to remain inside the Earth's atmosphere.

Global warming means that the increase in greenhouse gases released into the atmosphere prevents heat from leaving the Earth's atmosphere, causing a rise in the Earth's temperature. These gases are the result of…

- the burning of fossil fuels (oil, coal, gas) which produce carbon dioxide, sulphur dioxide and carbon monoxide, and contribute to **acid rain**
- motorised transportation burning petrol and diesel (which produces carbon dioxide, sulphur dioxide and carbon monoxide)
- an increase in cattle farming and rice growing: methane is released from wetlands (where rice grows) and from animals (particularly cattle)
- the use of CFCs (chlorofluorocarbons) in manufacturing processes
- deforestation: when trees grow, they take in carbon dioxide. If more and more trees are cut down, less carbon dioxide is removed from the atmosphere.

Monitoring of Global Warming

As the theory of global warming has become widely accepted, scientists need to monitor the impact that industrialisation has had on our planet. This is done by…

- monitoring the height of sea levels
- measuring the size of the polar ice sheets
- monitoring the salinity (salt concentration) of the oceans
- measuring how far glaciers have retreated
- monitoring changes to our climate from space.

(HT) Combating Global Warming

Although it is impossible to stop global warming there are ways in which we can fight it by…

- investing in and using new energy technologies which are renewable
- meeting the Kyoto protocol (an agreement between the developing countries to cut emissions of greenhouse gases by 5.2% by 2012) and getting developing nations to sign up to it (the US has yet to sign up)
- using geo-engineering to enhance plankton growth which takes in carbon (and therefore reduces the amount of carbon in the atmosphere).

All the methods of combating global warming are based on the **precautionary principle** that if we are not completely certain about the effects of something, we should act to prevent it.

Fractional Distillation of Crude Oil

Crude oil is a mixture of **hydrocarbons** (i.e. compounds containing hydrogen and carbon). The properties of the hydrocarbons in crude oil remain unchanged and specific. This makes it possible to separate the hydrocarbons in crude oil into their individual parts, or **fractions**, by **fractional distillation**.

The oil is evaporated by heating, then allowed to condense at a range of different temperatures to form fractions. Each resulting fraction contains hydrocarbon molecules with a similar number of carbon atoms. The process takes place in a fractionating column.

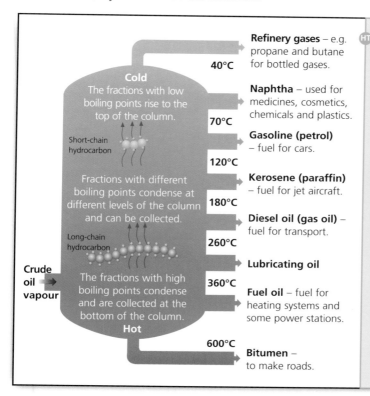

HT The larger the hydrocarbon (i.e. the greater the number of carbon atoms in a molecule)...
- the more viscous it is
- the less flammable it is
- the less volatile it is
- the higher its boiling point.

Hydrocarbon	No. of Carbon Atoms
Refinery gases	1–4
Naphtha	5–10
Gasoline	5–12
Kerosene	10–16
Diesel oil	15–22
Lubricating oil	20–30
Fuel oil	30–40
Bitumen	50+

Fractional Distillation of Air

Air is made up of three main gases: oxygen, nitrogen and carbon dioxide. We use oxygen in steel-making and nitrogen for quickly freezing food.

Both oxygen and nitrogen can be obtained by separating them from liquid air through **fractional distillation**.

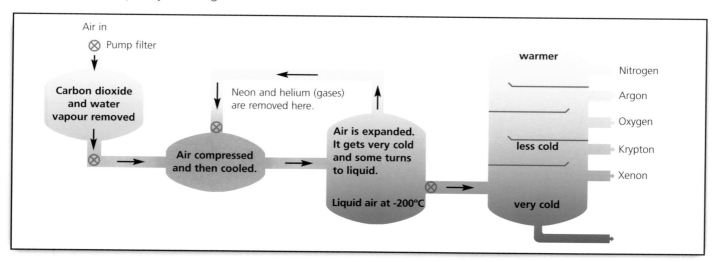

There's One Earth

Combustion of Fossil Fuels

A fuel is a substance that releases useful amounts of energy when burned. Many fuels are hydrocarbons.

When a fuel burns it reacts with oxygen from the air.

Fuels burn with differing flame colours, e.g. coal burns with a dirty yellow flame, methylated spirits burn with a purple flame.

Complete Combustion

When a hydrocarbon burns and there is plenty of oxygen available, complete combustion occurs, producing carbon dioxide and water, and releasing **energy**.

Methane	+	Oxygen	→	Carbon dioxide	+	Water
$CH_{4(g)}$	+	$2O_{2(g)}$	→	$CO_{2(g)}$	+	$2H_2O_{(l)}$

Incomplete Combustion

Sometimes a fuel burns without sufficient oxygen, e.g. in a room with poor ventilation. Then, incomplete combustion takes place. Instead of carbon dioxide being produced, carbon monoxide is formed.

Methane	+	Oxygen	→	Carbon monoxide	+	Water
$2CH_{4(g)}$	+	$3O_{2(g)}$	→	$2CO_{(g)}$	+	$4H_2O_{(l)}$

Incomplete combustion producing carbon monoxide can occur in faulty gas appliances and other heating appliances. This can be dangerous.

If there is *very* little oxygen available, carbon is produced. A sooty, yellow flame is an indication of incomplete combustion because it contains carbon which collects on the outside of a test tube containing water.

Methane	+	Oxygen	→	Carbon	+	Water
$CH_{4(g)}$	+	$O_{2(g)}$	→	$C_{(s)}$	+	$2H_2O_{(l)}$

With less oxygen…
- heat energy decreases
- pollutants and residue increase.

Although hydrocarbons produce useful amounts of energy when they burn, the gases they produce are pollutants:
- carbon dioxide increases the Greenhouse Effect and contributes to global warming
- carbon monoxide, a toxic, colourless and odourless gas combines irreversibly with the haemoglobin in red blood cells, reducing the oxygen carrying capacity of the blood (this eventually results in death through a lack of oxygen reaching body tissues)

- **HT** • other pollutants produced from burning fuels can have a serious impact on health and are thought by many to cause illnesses such as emphysema and asthma, which are notably more prevalent in developed countries.

Alternatives to Fossil Fuels

Bio-fuels are fast becoming an attractive alternative to fossil fuels. These are fuels based on sustainable resources such as animal waste, organic household waste, wood and alcohol. However, large areas of fertile land have to be used.

Alcohol in the form of ethanol can be fermented from sugar beet and sugar cane. It is a clean fuel as it only produces small amounts of carbon dioxide and water. However, lots of land is needed to grow the crops.

Ethanol	+	Oxygen	→	Carbon dioxide	+	Water
$C_2H_5OH_{(l)}$	+	$3O_{2(g)}$	→	$2CO_{2(g)}$	+	$3H_2O_{(g)}$

Hydrogen is the cleanest of all the fuels as it only produces water. If used in cars, it can supply three times the energy of petrol as well as being cheaper to run. However, new cars would be needed because of the technology used to get electricity from the hydrogen. Producing the hydrogen may involve the use of fossil fuels so could still add to pollution.

Recycling

When we recycle something that we no longer need, we find another use for it at the same time as conserving our planet's resources.

More and more materials can be recycled but the most common ones are metals, paper and glass.

Metals, when they are recycled, will use between $\frac{1}{20}$ and $\frac{1}{3}$ of the energy that they did the first time round. Aluminium and steel are currently the easiest metals to recycle.

Recycling paper reduces the amount of water and energy needed and the amount of methane released into the atmosphere.

Glass will not rot away. If it is recycled it takes 20% less energy than it did to make it in the first place, and produces 20% less pollution.

Economic and Environmental Considerations

Recycling makes environmental sense because it…
- saves on raw materials
- saves on landfill sites and other costs associated with waste disposal
- needs less energy than when the substance was first produced so it saves on fossil fuels
- cuts down on excavation and mining so there is less environmental damage and fewer waste products
- uses less water and chemicals so reduces pollution.

The more money an industry can save by recycling, then the more effort it will put in.

Recycling materials means there is **sustainability**.

Sustainable development is concerned with balancing the need for economic development, standards of living and respect for the environment, without compromising future generations. Sustainable resources are resources that can be maintained in the long term at a level that allows appropriate use by people.

Desalination

Desalination involves removing salt from salt water (e.g. sea water) to produce drinking water. It is used when the demand for fresh water is greater than the supply.

There's One Earth

Making Useful Substances

Getting salt and other useful products from sea water and rock salt involves a number of processes.

Sea water

1. The sea water is evaporated in wide shallow ponds to produce solar salt.
2. Solar salt is turned into saturated brine (salt water)
3. Saturated brine is boiled in vacuum pans to purify it.
4. The brine is left to evaporate leaving salt crystals.

Rock Salt (Sodium Chloride)

1. Rock salt is generally mined from the ground.
2. A process is then used which is similar to the process used to obtain salt from sea water.

The salt obtained from these processes is used in food production. However, the brine can be separated into other useful products.

Electrolysis of Sodium Chloride Solution

Sodium chloride (table salt) is used as a seasoning and preservative for foods, and in making pottery, soap, glass, textile dyes, and in chemical production.

If a direct current is passed through a concentrated solution of sodium chloride (rock salt) three main products are obtained:

- **Chlorine** at the positive electrode. This is used for making chemicals, bleaches, disinfectants, paints and plastics.
- **Hydrogen** at the negative electrode. This is used for manufacturing margarine and ammonia.
- **Sodium hydroxide** which remains in the solution and is used in making soap, paper and synthetic fibres.

Sodium is obtained from electrolysis of molten sodium chloride. This process also produces chlorine (see above for uses of chlorine).

Sodium is used in street lamps and in nuclear reactors, transferring heat from the reactor to the steam generators.

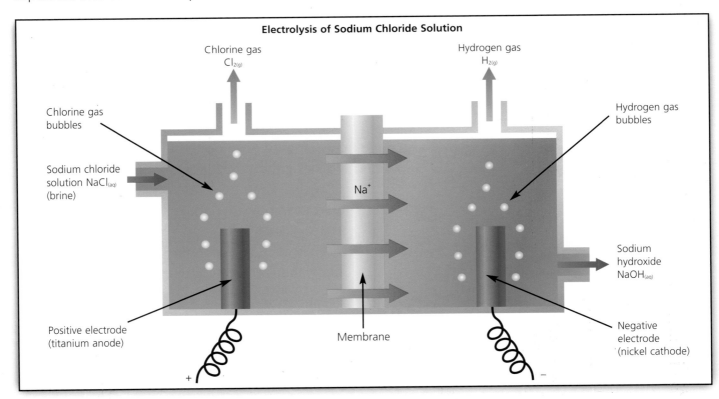

Electrolysis of Sodium Chloride Solution

Chlorine gas $Cl_{2(g)}$

Hydrogen gas $H_{2(g)}$

Chlorine gas bubbles

Hydrogen gas bubbles

Sodium chloride solution $NaCl_{(aq)}$ (brine)

Na^+

Sodium hydroxide $NaOH_{(aq)}$

Positive electrode (titanium anode)

Membrane

Negative electrode (nickel cathode)

+

−

There's One Earth

Glossary

Acid rain – rain that has reacted with gaseous pollutants in the air such as sulphur dioxide and nitrogen dioxide. The gases in the air are the result of the burning of fossil fuels

Bio-fuel – a source of renewable energy made from biological materials that include plants and animal waste

Combustion – a rapid oxidation reaction between a fuel and a gas (usually oxygen) releasing heat and, in most cases, light

Complete combustion – the production of carbon dioxide and water through the burning of a hydrocarbon

Crude oil – a mixture of hydrocarbon compounds which can be separated by fractional distillation. Crude oil is a fossil fuel

Desalination – the process of removing salt from water

Fossil fuels – natural sources of energy such as oil, coal and natural gas that have formed from the remains of plants and animals over millions of years

Fractional distillation – a method of separating a mixture of liquids which have different boiling points

Fractionating column – the equipment used to separate a mixture of liquids

Global warming – a rise in the average temperature of the Earth caused by an increase in the amount of carbon dioxide and other greenhouse gases released from burning fuels and deforestation

Hydrocarbons – compounds which are made only of hydrogen atoms and carbon atoms

Ignition – the means by which combustion is started

Incomplete combustion – this will happen if there is not enough oxygen when a fuel is being burned. It results in a sooty flame, carbon monoxide, carbon dioxide and water being produced

Recycle – to collect and reprocess an item for the purpose of remaking it as the same thing or as a different product

Residue – substances that are left behind after a reaction has taken place

Sootiness – the amount of carbon particles present in a flame: the more carbon particles there are, the greater the sootiness

Sustainability – the ability to meet the needs of the current generation without affecting the needs of future generations

Toxic – a substance that has the potential to kill a living organism

Viscosity – how easily a liquid can flow / be poured: if a liquid is highly viscous it is difficult to pour, e.g. treacle

Designer Products

Smart Materials

Smart materials are materials that are able to change their properties in response to an external stimulus. They are designed to react to heat, light and atmospheric conditions. Fabrics made from a smart material are designed to maximise characteristics such as lightness, breathability, waterproofing etc. Smart materials are usually manufactured using **microfibres** (very thin fibres of polymers) and have a variety of uses.

Smart Material	Information	Uses
Carbon fibre	• Carbon fibre strands or carbon fibre fabric are used to reinforce a variety of different polymers. The way the composite of carbon and polymer is made up will affect the product's properties. • Products made from carbon fibres are incredibly light and very strong. Some products are designed to be more flexible than metal.	• Carbon fibre is used for making items such as tennis rackets, hockey sticks, snowboards, paddles for water sports, and bicycles.
Thinsulate™	• Thinsulate is a unique insulation material made from microfibres. The microfibres trap more air than conventional fleece materials. • Thinsulate is a thin, warm, breathable, washable and dry-cleanable material. It is moisture-resistant and can keep you warm even when it is damp.	• Thinsulate is used for making outdoor clothing including dive-wear, ski-wear, mountaineering-wear and cycle-wear.
Lycra™	• Lycra is a unique man-made elastic fibre, also known as spandex. • It is always knitted or woven with other fabrics such as cotton, wool, silk and nylon. • The excellent stretch and recovery properties of Lycra produce fabrics and garments that are comfortable, fit well, and provide freedom of movement.	• Lycra is used to make swimwear, underwear, workout wear, running shorts, cycling shorts and other everyday clothing.

Designed Materials

Some **designed materials** can be considered to be the same type of material as a smart material. Products made from designed materials maximise the breathability, flexibility, waterproofing and lightness of the designed material. However, with some of these designed materials (e.g. Teflon and Post-its), it is only after they have been developed that a use for them becomes apparent.

Kevlar™

- Kevlar is a man-made organic fibre produced from a type of polymer called para-aramid.
- The unique properties of Kevlar come from the way the chains of polymer lay together within the structure of the material. There are many uses for this material because it is very strong and lightweight, it is hard to break and it is resistant to chemicals, cutting and fire.
- Uses include personal body armour, skis, helmets, kayaks, and aerospace and fire-protective clothing.

Teflon™

- Teflon was discovered in 1938 when a compressed sample of tetrafluoroethylene was found to have spontaneously polymerised into PTFE (polytetrafluorethylene), which was white and waxy.
- It is inert (unreactive) to virtually all chemicals and is considered to be the most slippery material in existence.
- It is most recognised today as the non-stick coating in cookware.

Post-its®

- Post-its use a special sticky material that was first discovered in 1968. But it was six years before Post-its were developed.
- This sticky material was special in that it had re-positionable properties.
- Post-its are now commonly used all over the world.

Gore-Tex™

- Gore-Tex is made from an expanded form of the polymer PTFE. Small amounts of the polymer are used to create a lattice-like structure.
- It is waterproof because the expanded PTFE is hydrophobic ('water hating').
- It is breathable because a hydrophilic ('water loving') substance is added to the structure that allows moisture to pass through.
- It can be laminated to another fabric using either heat or adhesive.
- Gore-Tex is used to make all-weather clothing and shoes, because it is waterproof and breathable.

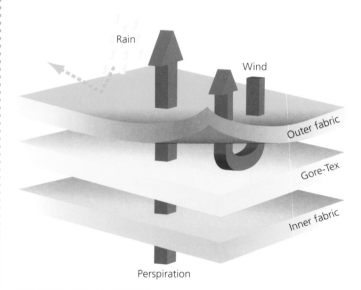

Designing New Products

An important part of product design is analysing how the product will be used and identifying all the properties it will need in order to perform its function effectively. Some properties are essential to enable the product to fulfil its purpose; others enhance the product and make it more desirable or useful. For example, windproof gloves for walkers must keep the wind out. However, there are other properties that will make them more comfortable to wear and user-friendly, e.g. being breathable, lightweight, flexible, warm, soft to the touch, washable, and being available in a variety of colours.

Designer Products

Nanotechnology

Nanotechnology is science which involves the study and the use of microscopically small materials. The term nano refers to the unit nanometre (nm), or 10^{-9} metres (which is approximately $\frac{1}{80\,000}$ of the width of a human hair!). On this tiny scale, materials exhibit much better properties than when they are larger.

Nanomaterials have properties that can be very useful in everyday items. Nanomaterials can be stronger and lighter than conventional materials, and can conduct heat or electricity in different ways.

Nanoparticles are incredibly tiny particles that have special applications. For example…

- tiny particles of titanium dioxide added to cosmetics and suntan lotions are transparent on the skin and can absorb or reflect UV (ultraviolet) radiation
- titanium dioxide can be layered onto the surface of glass to make self-cleaning windows. Using the properties of nanoparticles incorporated into the substance, the glass either repels water and dirt or breaks down accumulated dirt using UV rays and rain to wash the dirt off.

Nanocomposites

A composite is a substance that is made from a substance such as polymer (a chemical compound e.g. plastic) or concrete and a reinforcing material (e.g. glass fibre, carbon fibre and Kevlar). Composites are not chemically combined but the way they are put together produces a substance with improved properties.

Nanocomposites can be made from clay and polymer, metal and polymer, or carbon nanotube and polymer. The use of nanomaterials in composites will result in materials with many improved properties that can easily be changed by changing the size of the nanoparticles incorporated into the polymer. For example, nanocomposites can have…

- improved strength and thermal stability
- decreased permeability to liquids and gases
- composites that are more attractive to the consumer

- beneficial flame retardancy with reduced smoke emissions
- improved electrical conductivity and chemical resistance.

Future Uses of Nanotechnology

Scientists are constantly looking at what else they can use nanoparticles for, including…

- new generation army uniforms and equipment
- filters that can sterilise a wide range of drugs
- self-cleaning shoes, clothes, kitchen surfaces and bathroom tiles.

Nanotechnology has a lot of potential and is mostly aimed at medical uses such as diagnosis and drug delivery. For example, scientists are working on medical nanosensors that can be placed in cells to detect changes in chemical levels. This could be useful for studying diseases and general conditions.

HT Social and Ethical Issues

Although nanotechnology has great potential, there are social and ethical issues with any future uses of nanotechnology.

- Personal security and safety may be better due to the use of small sensors and computers. However, this could lead to the same technology being used to spy on people.
- Nanosensors could be used by the military to detect chemical and biological weapons. However, they could be used to create newer threats.
- Nanorobots could repair human bodies at the cellular level. However, people are worried that this is too unnatural.

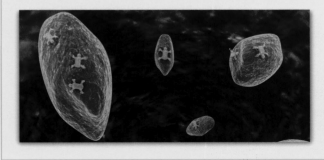

Intelligent Packaging

Intelligent packaging is packaging which has been specially developed to have properties which are desirable to the consumer. It uses similar technology to that already discussed on p.56. For example, some packages might include time-temperature food quality labels, self-heating or self-cooling containers for food, or cartons that contain electronic displays showing use-by dates.

Keeping Food Fresh

There are many different materials that are currently used in food packaging to help keep food fresh. For example, there are materials that can…

- soak up oxygen and help prevent food spoilage
- show whether perishable products have been stored at unsafe temperatures
- kill bacteria
- tell if food is about to go off
- remove moisture from the atmosphere of the package.

The 'Bullseye' Label (see alongside)

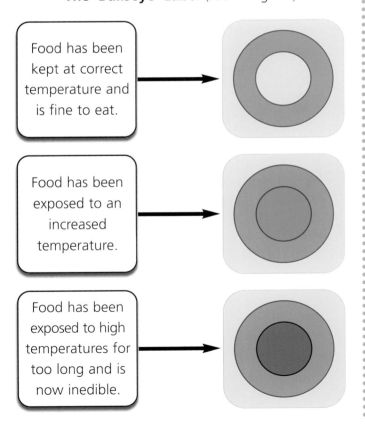

Food has been kept at correct temperature and is fine to eat.

Food has been exposed to an increased temperature.

Food has been exposed to high temperatures for too long and is now inedible.

Examples of Intelligent Packaging

The **'bullseye' label** is a time-temperature indicator. Consumers can see from the colour of the label whether the food has been kept at a warm temperature for too long.

- The central ring on the label contains chemicals that will polymerise over time.
- If the temperature is increased then the chemicals will polymerise quicker.
- This is shown by a change in colour from light to dark and indicates the growth of bacteria that will spoil the food.

The **'oxygen scavenger'** is an atmosphere controller. It removes oxygen from inside the package, preventing the decay of food. Currently, this is done by using a small sachet filled with modified iron (II) carbonate.

- This slows down decay of food and has the potential to extend the shelf life of perishable foods.
- It can improve food quality by reducing the need for additives and preservatives.
- Scientists are looking at the oxygen scavenger being incorporated into the film of the package by using multi-layer plastics.

Water in packaging can be minimised by the **absorption of liquid water**, or **humidity buffering**.

- Drip-absorbent sheets, often found in raw meat packages, absorb liquid water.
- Humidity buffering involves reducing the humidity inside the food package. This uses either a special multi-layer polymer film that is breathable to allow moisture to pass out but not in, or by using moisture-absorbing (desiccating) sachets. Common materials for the sachets are silica gel, calcium oxide, natural clays and molecular sieves.

Designer Products

Fermentation

Under the right temperature conditions, enzymes in **yeast** convert sugar into ethanol (alcohol) and carbon dioxide. This is **fermentation** and it can easily be demonstrated:

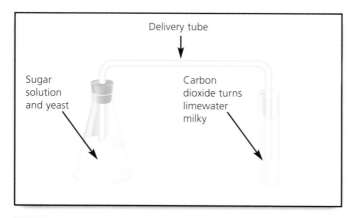

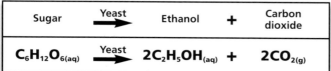

Sugar	$\xrightarrow{\text{Yeast}}$	Ethanol	+	Carbon dioxide
$C_6H_{12}O_{6(aq)}$	$\xrightarrow{\text{Yeast}}$	$2C_2H_5OH_{(aq)}$	+	$2CO_{2(g)}$

The ethanol produced during fermentation is used as the basis for the brewing and wine-making industries.

Yeast is added to the dough, and the carbon dioxide produced during fermentation is what makes the bread rise.

Alcohol and the Body

Ethanol is the form of alcohol which is found in alcoholic drinks. It can have many harmful effects on the body. Prolonged consumption of alcoholic drinks (ethanol) could result in these effects being permanent. Effects include…

- a deficiency in vitamin B causing skin damage, diarrhoea and depression
- decreased levels of iron, leading to anaemia
- liver damage: the liver would no longer be able to carry out its vital functions of making toxins safe
- destruction of brain cells
- an increased risk of cancer of the mouth, larynx, oesophagus, liver, stomach, colon, rectum and possibly the breast
- an increased risk of heart disease and high blood pressure
- inflammation and irritation of the intestinal and stomach lining leading to ulcers and damage to the pancreas
- in men, an inability to get an erection, shrinking testes and penis and a reduced sperm count
- in women, disruption to the menstrual cycle, risk of miscarriage and low birth weight or birth defects in their babies.

Alcohol and Society

There has been an increase in cases of binge drinking in the UK over recent years. Binge drinking is when a lot of alcohol is consumed in one session. This has many social implications, for example…

- hangovers
- mood changes which can be tearful or aggressive
- people finding themselves in violent situations (where perhaps they wouldn't if they hadn't been drinking)
- increased risk of accidents: wasting time / space in hospitals / doctors' surgeries
- lowered inhibitions mean greater risks of getting into trouble or doing things you regret afterwards.

Emulsifiers

An **emulsifier** is an additive which is put in food to stop the mixture of oil and water from separating. Normally oil and water do not mix, but when an emulsifier is added to the mixture, an **emulsion** is formed, e.g. mayonnaise. An emulsion can either be oil-in-water or water-in-oil:

- An oil-in-water emulsion contains small droplets of oil that are dispersed in water.
- A water-in-oil emulsion contains small droplets of water in oil.

How Emulsifiers Work

Emulsifiers keep the mixture of oil and water stable and stop it from separating into two layers. Emulsifiers are molecules that have two distinct ends: one end is **hydrophobic** ('water hating') and one end is **hydrophilic** ('water loving').

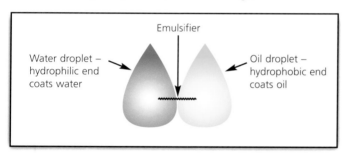

Emulsifier

Water droplet – hydrophilic end coats water

Oil droplet – hydrophobic end coats oil

In oil-in-water emulsions, the hydrophobic end hates water but loves oil so it will coat the oil molecules. The oil molecules become insulated from the water. This will prevent the oil-in-water emulsion from separating.

In water-in-oil emulsions, the hydrophilic end hates oil but loves water so it will coat the water molecules. The water molecules become insulated from the oil. This prevents the water-in-oil emulsion from separating.

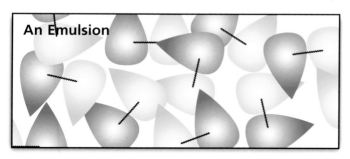

An Emulsion

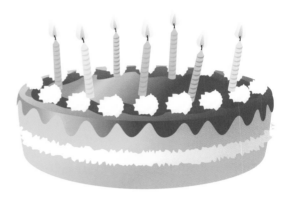

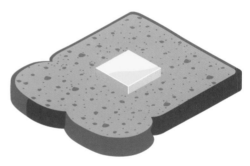

Uses of Emulsifiers in Food

- In bread, adding emulsifiers to the bread dough will stop the bread from developing large holes as it bakes.
- Low-fat spreads are water-in-oil emulsions so the emulsifier allows the oil and water to be mixed more easily.
- Ice cream and spray cream are types of aerated emulsion. The milk protein acts as a natural emulsifier but additional ones can be added to make the foam. An emulsifier helps the fat globules coat the small pockets of air so that the foam produced is stabilised.
- Sponge cakes use special emulsifiers to make tiny pockets of air producing an even structure and better volume in the finished cake.
- Emulsifiers are added to chocolate to stop the melted chocolate forming crystals or a white layer ('fat bloom') on the surface of the chocolate as it becomes solid again.

Designer Products

Glossary

Alcohol – a colourless, flammable liquid produced by fermentation of sugar solutions using enzymes in yeast

Breathability – the ability of a material to allow sweat vapours to escape from the inside of the fabric to the outside

Carbon fibre – a strong, stiff, thin fibre of nearly pure carbon which, when combined with other materials, produces a strong, lightweight material

Emulsifier – an additive that will stop two liquids from separating when they are mixed together, especially if those liquids would not normally mix together

Ethanol – a clear, colourless alcohol solution found in beverages such as wine, beer and brandy. It has the formula: C_2H_5OH

Fermentation – the name given to the process in which enzymes in yeast turn sugars (in particular glucose) into ethanol and carbon dioxide, without the need for oxygen

Gore-Tex™ – a brand of weatherproof membrane that allows small sweat particles to pass out from the body whilst preventing rain and wind from entering

Hydrophilic – a substance that will attract water, absorb water or dissolve in water

Hydrophobic – a substance that repels or 'hates' water, but attracts oil

Kevlar™ – a brand of aramid fibre that is strong, lightweight and flexible. It is often used to make bullet-resistant and stab-resistant vests

Lycra™ – a brand of spandex, a synthetic fibre, made from a long-chain polymer that has stretch and recovery properties giving comfort, fit and freedom of movement

Nanocomposites – composite materials made from particles less than 100 nanometres in size. They are materials that offer greater strength, wear and corrosion resistance than more traditional composites

Nanoparticles – very small particles that have at least one dimension less than 100 nanometres.

Nanotechnology – working with matter on an ultra-small scale in areas including medicine, physics, chemistry and engineering

Polymer – a long-chain hydrocarbon (compound of hydrogen and carbon), a plastic

Smart material – a material that senses its environment and responds to it. Examples can be found in food, packaging, sports and leisure

Sugar – a carbohydrate that is readily soluble in water. It is made during photosynthesis in plants and is found in many animals. It can also be turned into alcohol by enzymes in yeast

Teflon™ – a brand of polymer called PTFE (polytetrafluoroethene), a slippery non-stick material best-known for coating cookware

Thinsulate™ – a brand of thin, breathable fabric that is moisture-resistant and able to retain warmth whilst damp

Producing and Measuring Electricity

Types of Electric Current

Direct Current (d.c.)

Direct current flows in one direction only. Cells, batteries and solar cells are d.c.

1. Circuit drawings use arrows to show direct current flowing from + to -. (However, it is now known that electrons flow from - to +.)

2. On a cathode ray oscilloscope d.c. would look like this.

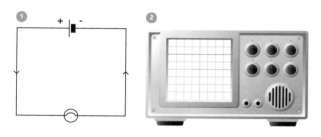

Alternating Current (a.c.)

Alternating current oscillates (reverses its direction) continuously. Mains electricity is a.c. (it has a frequency of 50 hertz).

1. 50 hertz means it oscillates 50 times per second. Because it changes direction, you cannot show the direction of a.c. using arrows.

2. On a cathode ray oscilloscope a.c. would look like this.

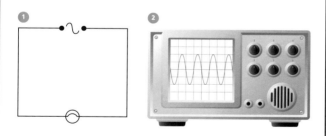

Cells and Batteries

Cells and **batteries** are sources of direct current. A single cell normally gives 1.5 volts. A battery contains two or more single cells (although single cells are commonly referred to as batteries). There are three main types of battery / cell:

Type	Contains	Used For...
Wet cell rechargeable	lead and acid	cars, industry
Dry cell non-rechargeable	zinc, carbon, manganese or mercury, lithium	torches, clocks, radios, hearing aids, pacemakers
Dry cell rechargeable	nickel, cadmium, lithium	mobile phones, power tools

Non-rechargeable batteries are not beneficial to the environment because...

- the energy needed to make a cell is 50 times greater than the energy it produces
- less than 5% of dry cells are recycled (compared to 90% of wet cell car batteries)
- the UK produces about 30 000 tonnes of waste dry cells every year (more than 20 cells per household)
- toxic chemicals like mercury, cadmium and lead can leak into the ground causing pollution.

Governments are starting to tackle this problem and various safe disposal (used batteries should not be placed in dustbins) and recycling schemes are being discussed. Rechargeable batteries are one alternative.

Advantages of Rechargeable Batteries

- Less expensive in the long run.
- Can be used many times over.
- Fewer batteries are discarded into the environment.
- Less of a drain on energy resources.

Disadvantages of Rechargeable Batteries

- Need to buy a charger.
- More expensive.
- Most contain carcinogenic (cancer-causing) chemicals.
- Can go 'flat' without warning (therefore unsuitable for smoke detectors etc.).

Producing and Measuring Electricity

Cells and Batteries (cont.)

The **capacity** of a battery is a measure of how much energy it can store and is given in units called **amp-hours (Ah)**. This information allows us to calculate how long a battery will work for before it goes 'flat' (uses all its stored energy). The higher the amp-hour rating, the more energy is stored in the battery.

1 amp-hour (Ah) = 1 amp (A) of electric current for 1 hour.

So, a battery capacity of 100Ah will provide:
   1A of current for 100 hours **or**
   100A of current for 1 hour **or**
   2A of current for 50 hours **or**
   4A of current for 25 hours, etc.

Capacity (Ah)	=	Current (A)	X	Hours (h)

Examples

Car battery   = 40Ah
              = 40 hours at 1A **or** 80 hours at 0.5A **or** 0.5 hours at 80A.

Torch battery = 2600mAh (milliamp-hours)
(1.5V AA type) = 2.6Ah
               = If working a 3W bulb it would use 2A and provide 1.3 hours of continuous use. (2 batteries would double the time to 2.6 hours.)

N.B. As a general rule, the heavier a lead acid battery is, the greater its capacity because it contains more lead.

Solar cells are also a source of electrical energy. They produce a direct current using the Sun's light energy.

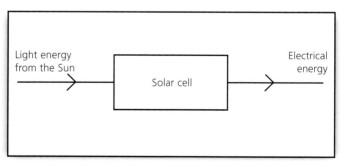

Light energy from the Sun → Solar cell → Electrical energy

Current

Electric current needs a complete circuit to flow. It will then flow continuously until the circuit is broken, e.g. a switch is opened (turned off).

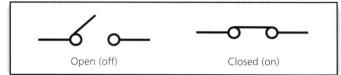

Open (off)   Closed (on)

Current is the rate of flow of **electrons** in a component. Electrons have a negative charge. In a complete circuit they leave the negative terminal because they are attracted towards the positive terminal. The greater the flow of electrons (i.e. the more electrons per second) the greater the current.

When current is flowing, energy is transferred from the cell to the circuit components (devices). The electric current will flow through an electrical component if there is a voltage (potential difference, p.d.) across the ends of the component.

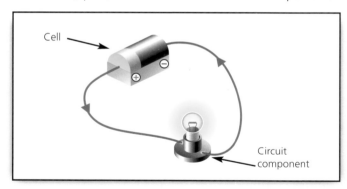

Cell

Circuit component

Voltage (Potential Difference, p.d.)

The atoms of all materials contain electrons but they are normally strongly bound by attraction to the positive nucleus of the atom. In metals (e.g. copper) some of the electrons are less tightly bound (free electrons) and are able to move between the atoms within the metal, making metals good conductors.

When a conductor (e.g. a piece of copper wire) is connected to a d.c. supply, the **voltage (potential difference)** drives the electrons along the conductor. This is an electric current. The greater the potential difference, the greater the electron flow (or 'drift') and the greater the current.

Producing and Measuring Electricity

Measuring Current and Voltage

Current (the measure of electron flow) is measured using an **ammeter** in units called **amperes (amps, A)**. The milliamp (mA) is used for very small currents. 1mA = 0.001A (1/1000A).

At any point in a series circuit, the rate of electron flow will be the same, so the current and ammeter readings will be the same.

Voltage (the measure of electrical force) is measured in **volts** using a **voltmeter**. Voltmeters must be connected across a component (i.e. in parallel).

Current and voltage can be measured at the same time.

Circuit Symbols

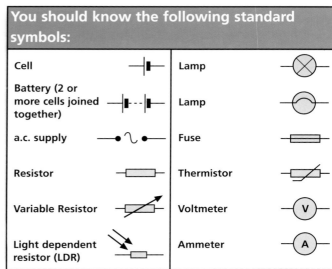

You should know the following standard symbols:

Cell		Lamp	
Battery (2 or more cells joined together)		Lamp	
a.c. supply		Fuse	
Resistor		Thermistor	
Variable Resistor		Voltmeter	
Light dependent resistor (LDR)		Ammeter	

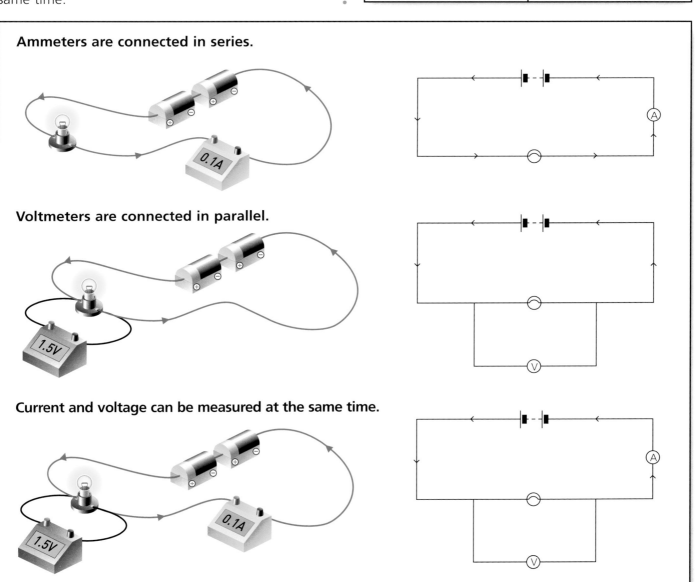

Ammeters are connected in series.

Voltmeters are connected in parallel.

Current and voltage can be measured at the same time.

Producing and Measuring Electricity

Making Electricity by Electromagnetic Induction

If you move a wire (or coil of wire) so that it cuts through a magnetic field (through the lines of force), then a voltage is induced between the ends of the wire. This will cause electrons to flow along the wire creating an electric current, if the wire is part of a complete circuit.

Moving the wire into the magnetic field induces a current in one direction.

Moving the wire out of the magnetic field induces a current in the opposite direction.

If there is no movement of the wire, there is no induced current.

The same effect can be seen using a coil and a magnet.

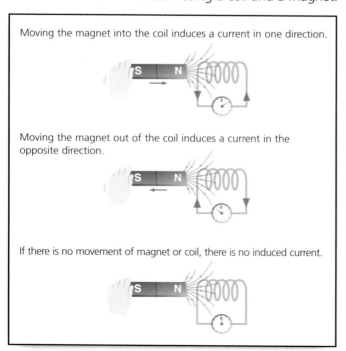

Moving the magnet into the coil induces a current in one direction.

Moving the magnet out of the coil induces a current in the opposite direction.

If there is no movement of magnet or coil, there is no induced current.

Increasing Voltage and Current

A coil of wire is rotated in a magnetic field. As the coil cuts through the magnetic field, a current is induced in the wire. This current reverses direction every half turn. To increase the voltage it is necessary to cut through more magnetic field lines per second. This can be done by…

- having stronger magnets
- having more coils of wire
- moving the wire (or magnet) faster

Generators use the principle of moving (rotating) coils of wire in a magnetic field to generate electricity; a coil of wire cuts through a magnetic field to induce a voltage.

The same effects can be achieved by rotating a magnet within a coil of wire. This is used in a **bicycle dynamo** (generator) to generate electricity for the bicycle's lights.

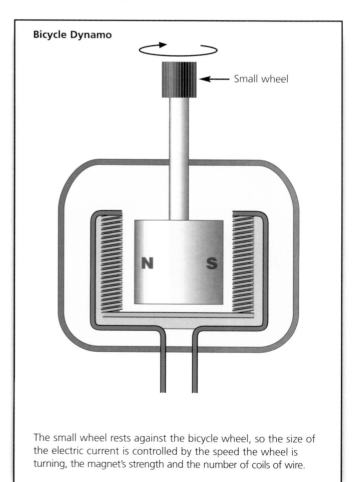

Bicycle Dynamo

Small wheel

The small wheel rests against the bicycle wheel, so the size of the electric current is controlled by the speed the wheel is turning, the magnet's strength and the number of coils of wire.

Producing and Measuring Electricity

Resistance

Resistance is a measure of how hard it is for a current to flow through a conductor. Resistance is measured in **ohms** (Ω).

For most materials, resistance increases in proportion to an increase in temperature. For example, if a light bulb is going to stop working, it normally 'blows' when it is switched on. This is because it is cold so it has a low resistance, which gives a higher current. The high current makes the filament / wire so hot it melts, breaking the circuit.

Thermistors (see below right) work in the opposite way: they are inversely proportional. Their resistance decreases as the temperature increases.

All components have resistance. The bigger the resistance of a component (or components), the smaller the current that flows for a particular voltage.

Two lamps together have a bigger resistance than one lamp on its own. This means a smaller current flows, causing the lamps to produce a dimmer light.

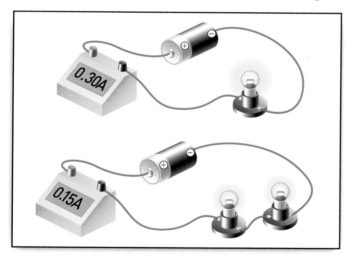

A **resistor** is a component which has a fixed resistance. When an electric current passes through a resistor, the moving electrons collide with atoms within the resistor, giving up their energy. This results in the temperature of the resistor increasing.

Three common electrical appliances which use this effect are hairdryers, immersion heaters, toasters and light bulbs.

Light-dependent Resistor and Thermistor

Light-dependent resistors and thermistors are components whose resistance depends on the surrounding external conditions.

Light-dependent resistor (LDR)

The resistance of an LDR depends on light intensity. Its resistance decreases as light intensity increases.

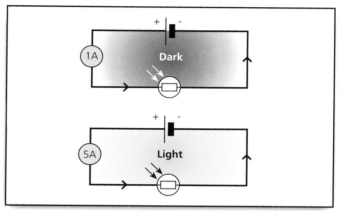

Uses of LDRs: automatic light detectors (e.g. to switch on a light when it gets dark; controlling the exposure time (how long the shutter is open) of a digital camera – in poor light the shutter needs to be open for longer.

Thermistor

The resistance of a thermistor depends on its temperature. Its resistance decreases as the temperature of the thermistor increases.

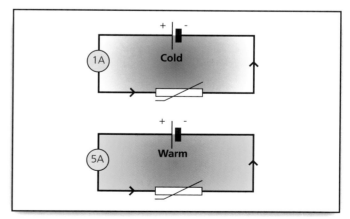

Uses of Thermistors: automatic temperature detectors (e.g. frost detectors, fire alarms); measuring engine temperatures of cars (shown on the temperature gauge).

Producing and Measuring Electricity

Current, Voltage and Resistance

Each part of a circuit tries to resist the flow of electrons (current). Even good conductors, like copper wire, have resistance but it is so low it can normally be ignored.

Insulators have resistances which are so large that, under normal circumstances, current cannot flow.

As more components are added into a series circuit, the resistance increases. However, this is not true for a parallel circuit, because in a parallel circuit, each component has its own loop connected to the battery terminal.

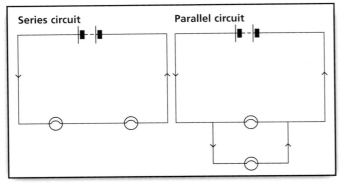

As a greater voltage is supplied to a series circuit, the current increases which makes the bulbs brighter.

The greater the resistance the smaller the current. The larger the voltage the greater the current.

Resistance, voltage and current are related by the following formula:

| Voltage (volts, V) | = | Current (ampere, A) | X | Resistance (ohm, Ω) |

$$\frac{V}{I \times R}$$

where I is current

So, to find the resistance of a component, measure the current flowing through it and the voltage across it. In the following circuit, the voltage is 3 volts and the current 0.2 amps. The lamp's resistance is…

$$\text{Resistance} = \frac{\text{Voltage}}{\text{Current}}$$

$$R = \frac{3}{0.2} = 15 \text{ ohms}$$

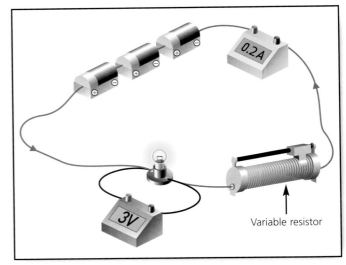

Variable resistor

A **variable resistor** is a component whose resistance can be altered. By altering the resistance, we can change the current that flows through a component, and the voltage across a component. This enables a range of outputs to be possible, e.g. greater volume, brighter light.

From the voltage–current–resistance triangle (below left), three equations can be obtained:

Example 1

Find the voltage needed across a conductor of resistance 50 Ω to cause a current of 2A to pass through it.

$$V = IR \quad V = 2 \times 50 \quad = 100V$$

Example 2

A potential difference of 12V is put across a conductor of resistance 24 Ω. Find the current that flows through the resistor.

$$I = \frac{V}{R} \quad I = \frac{12}{24} = 0.5A$$

Example 3

A potential difference of 24V placed across a conductor causes a current of 0.2A to flow through the conductor. What is the conductor's resistance?

$$R = \frac{V}{I} \quad R = \frac{24}{0.2} = 120 \Omega$$

Producing and Measuring Electricity

Current–Voltage Graphs

Current–voltage graphs show how the current through a component varies with the voltage across it. If we include a **variable resistor** (rheostat) in our circuit, we can get a range of current and voltage readings which are needed to plot a graph.

If the component is kept at a constant temperature the current is directly proportional to the voltage and the graph will be a straight line of current against voltage. If it is not kept at a constant temperature, the graph will be curved.

Examples for Various Components

1 Resistor

If the temperature of the resistor remains constant, equal increases in voltage across the resistor will produce equal increases in current through the resistor, giving a straight line.

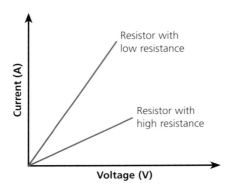

2 Wires made of different metals

This is the same as the resistor example (alongside), as long as the temperature of the wires remains constant. (Assume that both wires are identical in length and diameter.)

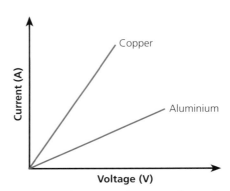

N.B. Copper has a lower resistance than aluminium.

3 Filament bulb

As the bulb gets hotter, the resistance increases. Look at the dotted lines: equal increases in voltage give smaller increases in current.

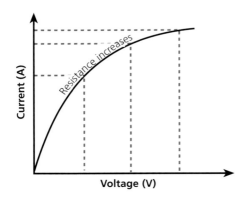

4 Thermistor

As the thermistor gets hotter, the resistance decreases. A small increase in voltage gives a large increase in current. (See how the current lines are spaced further apart than the voltage lines.)

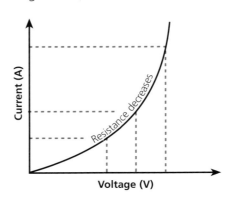

Producing and Measuring Electricity

Electricity and the Modern World

Electricity has had a huge impact on the making of the modern world. Think of everything you use that depends on electricity.

Device	Invented
Electric Iron	1882
Electric Kettle	1891
Electric Fire	1892
Vacuum Cleaner	1908
Television	1920s

When they were first made, these devices were very uncommon because of their cost and the lack of electricity supply. In 1920 only 10% of homes had an electricity supply.

The electric telephone, invented by Alexander Graham Bell in 1876, used only a small amount of electricity which could be supplied along the phone line, so mains electricity was not essential. It was the beginning of modern electrical communications.

Computer Technology

The invention of the microchip, on which integrated circuits could be built, led to modern computers.

Computers store data as 0s and 1s, which depend on electrical switches being off (0) or on (1). It is how these switches are made that affects the size and speed of the computer.

An integrated circuit can have the equivalent of millions of transistors in a tiny space; the components are very close, so the speed is increased. Computer circuits must be as small as possible so that the electrical switches are turned on and off quickly and with less work.

Future uses for very small electric circuits could include...
* medical monitoring (to constantly display patients' pulse rate etc.)
* very small, thin watches, phones etc. worn like sticking plasters.

Superconductivity

In 1911, Onnes discovered that when materials cooled to certain temperatures, they had zero resistance, or **'superconductivity'**. Currently, zero resistance only occurs at very low temperatures but research is being carried out to achieve superconductivity at higher temperatures.

In 1933, Meissner discovered that superconductors expelled magnetic flux from within them. So, when placed with a strong magnet, the magnetic fields opposed and produced a current in the superconductor.

The **Maglev train**, proposed in 1934, was based on superconductivity. (Maglev is short for magnetic levitation.) Maglev trains are moved along by electromagnets. Electrified coils in the walls and track create a magnetic field which propels the train. The magnetised coil running along the track repels the large magnets on the train's undercarriage, allowing it to levitate (float). Power is supplied to the coils within the track walls to create magnetic fields that pull / push the train along. This eliminates friction and allows the train to travel at over 500 km/h.

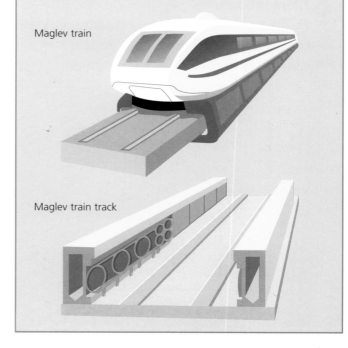

Maglev train

Maglev train track

Glossary

Ammeter – an instrument used to measure electric current

Amperes / Amps (A) – the unit used to measure electric current

Battery – a device that uses a chemical reaction to generate electricity

Capacity – a measure of how much energy a battery is able to store. It is normally measured in amp-hours (Ah)

Circuit – a complete loop, containing electrical components, between the two terminals of a power supply

Current – the rate of flow of electrons through a conductor

Dry cell – the most common type of battery; a battery which contains no liquid, but it does need a paste between the positive and negative terminals

Dynamo – a device for generating electricity from the simple rotational motion of a coil in a magnetic field or the rotation of a magnet inside a coil

Light-dependent resistor (LDR) – an electronic component whose resistance varies with light intensity

Magnet – a magnetised piece of metal surrounded by a magnetic field

Milliamps (mA) – 0.001 or $\frac{1}{1000}$ of an amp. 1000mA = 1A

Millivolts (mV) – 0.001 or $\frac{1}{1000}$ of a volt. 1000mV = 1V

Ohms (Ω) – the unit of electrical resistance. 1 ohm is the resistance of a conducting material across which a potential difference of 1V causes a current of 1A to flow

Rechargeable – a battery which is able to have its chemical energy replaced

Resistance – the property of materials to resist the flow of electric current through them (to a lesser or greater degree)

Resistor – an electronic component designed to produce a known (fixed) resistance

Series – a type of circuit in which all the components are connected in one continuous loop, with a common current running through them all

Solar cell – a device which is able to transform light energy into electrical energy

Thermistor – an electronic component whose resistance varies with temperature

Voltage – the value of the potential difference between two points, e.g. the terminals of a cell

Volts (V) – the unit of potential difference

> **HT** **Superconductivity** – a property of materials that have no resistance to electric current at low temperatures

You're in Charge

Electricity from Renewable Energy Sources

Electricity is a secondary source of energy: it needs a primary source of energy, such as wind or waves, to produce it. Wind and waves are **renewable energy sources** because they will not run out.

Coal power stations generate electricity by burning coal to heat water and produce steam which drives turbines and rotates a generator. Coal is a **non-renewable energy source**. All renewable energy sources (except solar) produce electricity by driving turbines directly.

Using any renewable energy source will have an economic, environmental and social impact. For example, many of the renewable energy sources have high initial set-up costs and change the appearance of their surroundings. However, they provide electricity without producing atmospheric pollution.

Some of the major advantages (**+**) and disadvantages (**-**) of using renewable energy sources are given below, and on the following two pages.

Wind

The force of the wind turns the blades of a wind turbine, causing a generator to spin and produce electricity.

+ Does not produce waste or atmospheric pollution.
+ Free energy source.
− Equipment is expensive to install.
− Low output per turbine.
− Wind is unreliable.
− Visual pollution.

Propeller blades

Wind

Generator

Tidal

At high tide water is trapped by a barrage. At low tide the water is released back to the same level as the sea. The water's movement drives a turbine to generate electricity.

+ Does not produce waste or atmospheric pollution.
+ Free energy source.
+ Reliable (high and low tide are regular).
+ High output: operates almost continuously.
− Spoils appearance of river.
− Interferes with river traffic.
− Damages habitats.

Water at high tide

Barrage

Turbines

You're in Charge

Waves

The motion of the waves makes the nodding duck move up and down. This movement is translated into a rotary movement which turns a generator to produce electricity.

+ Does not produce waste or atmospheric pollution.
+ Free energy source.
− Equipment expensive to install.
− Variable wave size means unreliable, low output.
− Changes appearance of coastline and is a danger to ships.

Hydro-electric

Water stored in reservoirs above the power station flows down to drive turbines to generate electricity. It is pumped back up when demand is low.

+ Does not produce waste or atmospheric pollution.
+ Reliable and free energy source.
+ Fast response; can support the National Grid during high demand.
+ High output: the water can be used many times.
− Damages habitats and villages.
− Requires high rainfall and mountainous region.
− Changes appearance of surroundings.

Geothermal

In some volcanic areas hot water and steam rise naturally, having been heated up by the decay of radioactive substances within the Earth. The steam can be used to drive turbines.

+ Does not produce waste or atmospheric pollution.
+ Free energy source.
+ Can be used as a source of hot water if not generating electricity.
− Expensive to install and maintain.
− Few suitable sites.
− Low output.

73

You're in Charge

Solar Power

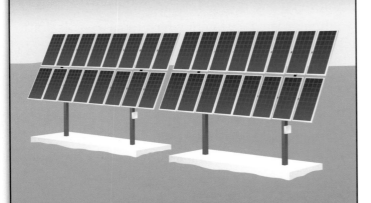

Solar cells use modern technology to transfer sunlight directly into useful electricity, e.g. in calculators, watches and garden lighting, as well as more sophisticated uses in space probes and satellites.

+ Does not produce waste or atmospheric pollution.
+ Can be used on very small scale, e.g. calculators.
+ No need for turbines and generators.
+ Can be very light, easily portable.
+ Free energy source.
− Can only operate during daylight hours.

Light in / Electrical energy out

Biomass / Wood

Wood can be classed as a renewable energy source: trees can be grown relatively quickly to replace those which are burnt to provide energy. Wood can also be used to heat water to produce steam to rotate a turbine and generator.

+ Widely available source.
− Produces smoke and waste.
− Costly: trees need cutting, transporting and replanting as soon as they are cut down.
− Changes the landscape.
− Releases carbon dioxide into the air.

The Future for Energy

There needs to be an overall strategy for future electricity production which involves…

- more efficient use of current sources (if every light bulb in the UK was replaced with a low energy bulb, two power stations would no longer be needed)
- an integration of traditional non-renewable sources (coal, oil, gas and nuclear) with renewable sources.

The non-renewable energy sources are major polluters and contributors to global warming, and will eventually run out. But, if renewable sources are going to work, people must change their attitudes towards visual pollution and accept the high initial costs.

The **National Grid** collects electrical energy generated in power stations and distributes it. As more smaller systems (e.g. renewable sources) generate and contribute to the National Grid, careful thought will be required for a modernised system.

Scientific knowledge and understanding have led to the development of new technologies (e.g. in medicine), which have a huge impact on society.

Scientific ideas change and develop over time. The scientific knowledge, and technologies, that we have today are the product of thousands of years of observation, questioning and investigation. The process by which scientific ideas develop can be summarised as below.

A phenomenon is observed.

Scientists develop hypotheses or theories based on the observation and current scientific knowledge.

Research and investigations are carried out to test the hypotheses and theories.

The results are analysed and conclusions are drawn.

The hypotheses or theories are discounted, changed or refined.

As scientific understanding in one field grows and develops, it often enables growth and development to take place in other related areas of science.

Example
The timeline opposite looks at how key discoveries in electricity have enabled the development of electrotherapy in medicine, i.e. the use of electric current for pain relief and to aid healing.

In the future, our understanding of electricity and its effects on the body will continue to develop and, as a result, our technologies should become safer and more efficient.

1745 – The first electrical capacitor was invented, allowing static electricity to be accumulated and enabling studies into electricity.

1746 – Jean Jallabert discovered that muscles could be stimulated using electricity, and successfully treated a paralysed patient using a capacitor to electrify him.

1781 – Having studied frogs legs, Luigi Galvani deduced that muscle contractions were caused by electricity flowing through nerves. This suggested that electricity *could* be used in medical treatments.

1804 – Charles Wilkinson published guidelines for using electrical currents to treat certain conditions. Tetanus, tumours and paralysis are all still treated with electricity today.

1820-1831 – Studies led to an understanding of electromagnetic induction and the development of generators that provided a steady supply of electricity for medical use.

1860s – A current from an induction coil was used to diagnose the causes of conditions like paralysis.

1890s – Jacques d'Arsonval discovered that increasing current frequency reduced the pain caused. Heinrich Hertz invented a machine which generated high-frequency currents, so pain-free applications became possible. Hertz's invention also revealed that high-frequency currents could destroy tumours and had an anaesthetic effect, which helped to relieve chronic rheumatism, nervous conditions and neuralgic pains.

1970s – A device called TENS (Transcutaneous Electrical Nerve Stimulation) was developed. It uses electrical impulses to block pain signals in the nerves. One application is during childbirth.

2000 – EMS (Electrical Muscle Stimulation) was used to help a person paralysed from the neck down to regain some sensation and movement.

The Simple (d.c.) Electric Motor

Electric motors form the basis of a vast range of electrical devices both inside and outside of the home.

As current flows through the coil, each side creates a magnetic field which interacts with the permanent magnetic field of the magnet. A force acts on both sides of the coil which rotates it.

In order to keep the coil rotating continuously the current has to reverse its direction of flow every half turn. This is done using the split-ring **commutator**.

1. Each end of the coil is connected to one half of the commutator. An electric current flows in through one half of the commutator via the carbon brushes, passes through the coil, then flows out through the other half of the commutator causing the coil to rotate.
2. As the coil rotates it reaches a vertical position. No current flows through it because the commutator no longer makes contact with the brushes; each section of the commutator is separated by an insulator.
3. However, the coil rotates past this vertical position due to its own momentum. The direction of the current through the coil now changes due to the split-ring commutator. This causes the coil to continually rotate in the same direction because the current reverses its direction of flow through the coil every half turn.

Reversing the Direction of Rotation

There are two ways to reverse the direction of rotation:

1. reverse the direction of the current around the coil by reversing the power supply to the brushes.
2. reverse the magnetic field.

A Real Electric Motor

Real motors have several separate coils of wire wrapped around the armature, each with its own pair of commutator segments.

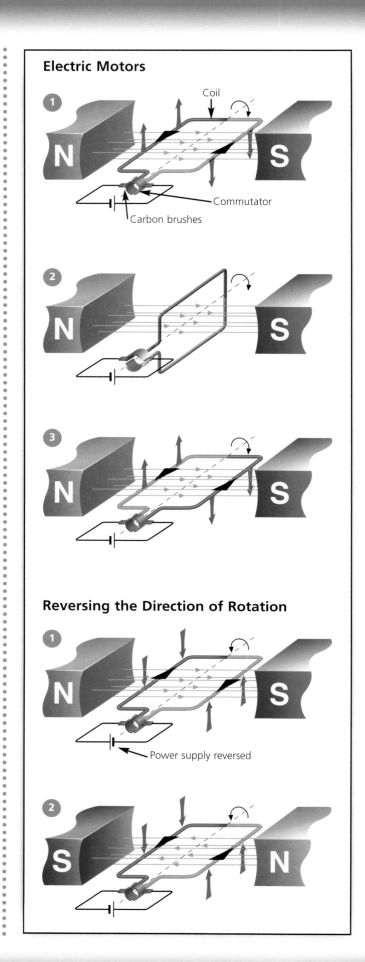

Electric Motors

1 — Coil, Commutator, Carbon brushes

Reversing the Direction of Rotation

1 — Power supply reversed

Electrical Power

Electrical energy is transferred to an appliance by electric current through a cable. The appliance then transforms the electrical energy into other forms (e.g. light, sound). Some energy will always be 'lost' as heat in the cable.

The **power** of an appliance is determined by the rate at which electrical energy is transferred. This is measured in **joules per second** (J/s).

Calculating Power

The power of an appliance is calculated using the formula:

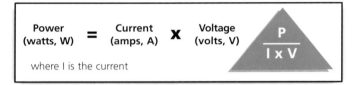

| Power (watts, W) | = | Current (amps, A) | X | Voltage (volts, V) | $\frac{P}{I \times V}$ |

where I is the current

1 watt is the transfer of 1 joule of energy in 1 second. For example, a computer monitor with a power rating of 200W transfers 200 J/s.

Most appliances have a label on them which gives the power and the voltage, so we can work out the current and, therefore, the fuse needed.

Example 1

Calculate the fuse needed for the iron.

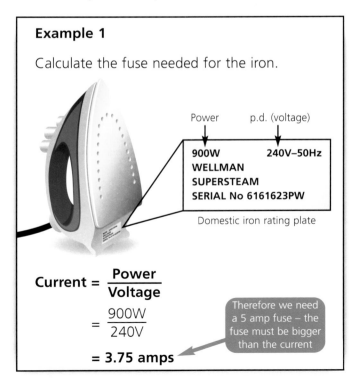

Power p.d. (voltage)

900W 240V–50Hz
WELLMAN
SUPERSTEAM
SERIAL No 6161623PW

Domestic iron rating plate

$$\text{Current} = \frac{\text{Power}}{\text{Voltage}}$$

$$= \frac{900W}{240V}$$

Therefore we need a 5 amp fuse – the fuse must be bigger than the current

$$= 3.75 \text{ amps}$$

Example 2

A 1.2kW electric fire works best using 5A of current. What should be the voltage of its supply?

(1.2kw = 1 200W)

$$V = \frac{P}{I} \qquad V = \frac{1\ 200}{5} = 240 \text{ volts}$$

If an appliance transfers more electrical energy than another appliance it will cost more to use for the same time period. Energy from the mains supply is measured in kilowatt-hours (kWh), often called a unit. If an electrical appliance transfers 1kWh of energy, it transfers 1 kilowatt (1000W) of power in 1 hour.

Examples

Time must be in hours. Power must be in kW.

A 200W (0.2kW) television transfers 1kWh of energy if it is switched on for 5 hours.
0.2kW x 5 hours = 1kWh

A 2000W (2kW) kettle transfers 1kWh of energy if it is switched on for $\frac{1}{2}$ hour (30 mins).
2kW x $\frac{1}{2}$ hour = 1kWh

To calculate the cost, we need to use the formula:

| Cost | = | Power | X | Time | X | Cost of 1kWh |

Example

A 2000W electric hot plate was used for 90 minutes. How much did it cost to use if 1kWh (unit) costs 7p?
2000W = 2.0kW. 90 minutes = 1.5 hours.

Cost = power x time x cost of 1kWh
= 2 x 1.5 x 7p
= 21p

You're in Charge

Efficiency

When devices transfer energy, only part of it is usefully transferred to where it is wanted and in the form that is wanted. The remainder is 'wasted'.

The amount of useful energy transferred by an appliance is called the **efficiency** of the appliance and is calculated using:

$$\text{Efficiency} = \frac{\text{Useful output}}{\text{Total input}} \times 100\%$$

N.B. No device can have an efficiency greater than 100%.

Example – Electric Kettle

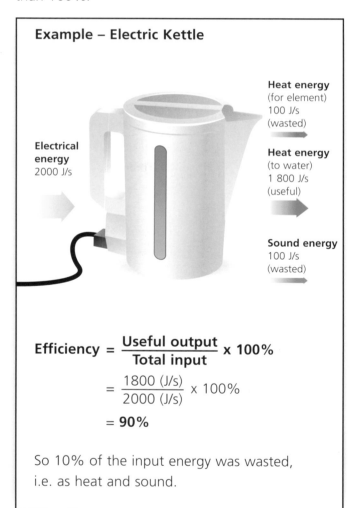

Electrical energy 2000 J/s

Heat energy (for element) 100 J/s (wasted)

Heat energy (to water) 1 800 J/s (useful)

Sound energy 100 J/s (wasted)

$$\text{Efficiency} = \frac{\text{Useful output}}{\text{Total input}} \times 100\%$$

$$= \frac{1800 \ (\text{J/s})}{2000 \ (\text{J/s})} \times 100\%$$

$$= \mathbf{90\%}$$

So 10% of the input energy was wasted, i.e. as heat and sound.

The total amount of energy before the transfer is equal to the total amount of energy after the transfer. This is called the **principle of conservation of energy** and is true for any appliance that transfers energy.

Efficiency of Solar Cells

Solar cells are not very efficient devices. The efficiency of transferring light energy from the Sun into electrical energy from the solar cell used to be generally less than 20%. Scientists in the space industry have increased efficiency to over 40% in research conditions.

Solar cells are currently used in sunny areas or remote places where it is more difficult to get other forms of electrical supply. Increasing efficiency, so they can operate effectively with less sunlight, is the key to making them usable across the world.

House Insulation

It is important to insulate houses so that less energy is required to heat them. This means less of the world's energy resources are used and fuel bills are cheaper. It costs money to install insulation, so in order to compare energy saving measures we calculate the payback time.

$$\text{Payback time} = \frac{\text{Installation cost}}{\text{Annual saving}}$$

Type of Insulation	Approximate Payback Time (Years)
Covering hot water tank	0.5
Draught proofing	2
Loft insulation	2
Wall insulation	5
Double glazing	20

Mains Electricity

3-Pin Plug

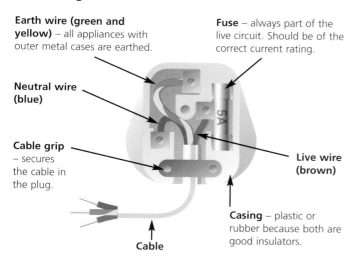

Earth wire (green and yellow) – all appliances with outer metal cases are earthed.

Fuse – always part of the live circuit. Should be of the correct current rating.

Neutral wire (blue)

Cable grip – secures the cable in the plug.

Live wire (brown)

Casing – plastic or rubber because both are good insulators.

Cable

The alternating current passes to the connected appliance via the neutral and live wires.

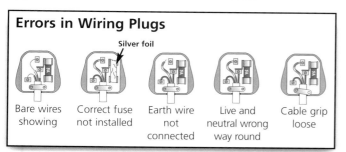

Errors in Wiring Plugs

Silver foil

Bare wires showing | Correct fuse not installed | Earth wire not connected | Live and neutral wrong way round | Cable grip loose

Fuses

A **fuse** is a short, thin piece of wire with a low melting point. When the current passing through it exceeds the fuse's current rating, the fuse wire gets hot and melts / breaks, preventing damage to the cable, appliance, and user.

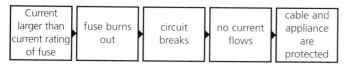

Current larger than current rating of fuse → fuse burns out → circuit breaks → no current flows → cable and appliance are protected

For this safety system to work properly, the current rating of the fuse must be just above the normal working current of the appliance.

Some appliances are **double insulated**: all metal parts inside the appliance are completely insulated from any outer part of the appliance which may be handled. These appliances do not have an earth wire but they are still protected by a fuse.

Earthing

All electrical appliances with outer metal cases must be **earthed**. The outer case of the appliance is connected to the earth pin in the plug through the earth wire. When the current is below the current rating of the fuse the appliance works properly.

However, if a fault in the appliance connects the live wire to the case, then the case will become live. This current will 'run to earth' through the earth wire because this offers less resistance and this overload of current will cause the fuse wire to melt.

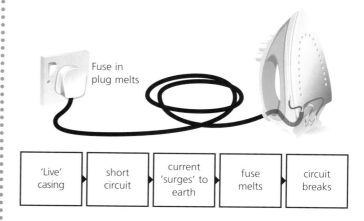

Fuse in plug melts

'Live' casing → short circuit → current 'surges' to earth → fuse melts → circuit breaks

Residual Current Circuit Breakers (RCCBs)

Most modern houses have **circuit breakers**. A circuit breaker depends on an electromagnet which separates a pair of contacts when the current becomes high enough. Each circuit (e.g. downstairs lights) will have its own RCCB.

Advantages of RCCBs (compared with fuses):
- They are safer – less physical contact, do not get hot.
- They react more quickly to a fault.
- It is easier to switch off certain circuits for repairs.
- It is easy to see which circuit a fault has occurred in.
- They are easy to reset (once the fault has been corrected) – press a button rather than replace a fuse.

You're in Charge

Glossary

Earth wire – a wire that connects an appliance to the earth (ground), normally via a plug and socket

Efficiency – the ratio of the useful energy obtained from a device compared to the amount of energy put into the device to operate it

Electricity – electric current used as a source of power

Energy – the ability to do work. It can be transferred from one place to another (e.g. along a wire) as electrical energy and transformed into other types (e.g. from electrical to light), but it cannot be created or destroyed, i.e. there is a fixed amount

Fuse – a device containing a thin piece of wire that protects appliances by melting and putting a gap in a circuit if the current becomes too high

Insulation – a material used to reduce the transfer of heat energy

Joules (J) – the unit of energy

Millivolts (mV) – 0.001V or $\frac{1}{1000}$ of a volt. 1000mV = 1V

Motor – a device used for producing kinetic energy from a power source, normally as the result of a current flowing around a coil situated in a magnetic field

Power – the rate at which work is done or energy is transferred by a device

Solar cell – a device that is able to convert light energy directly into electrical energy

Solar power – the power from the Sun's radiation

Voltage – the value of the potential difference between two points, e.g. the terminals of a cell

Volts (V) – the unit of potential difference

Watts / kilowatts (W/kW) – the unit of power, equals the rate of transfer of 1J of energy per second. 1kilowatt (kW) = 1000W

Wind power – power produced from the motion of the wind, e.g. by a wind turbine

HT Residual Current Circuit Breakers (RCCB) – an electromagnetic device which puts a gap in a circuit by separating two contacts if the current exceeds a safe value

Now You See It, Now You Don't

Waves

Waves are a regular pattern of disturbance. They transfer energy from one point to another without any transfer of matter. Waves can be produced in ropes, springs and on the surface of water.

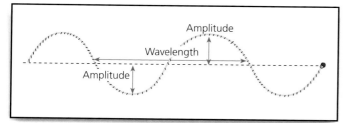

- **Amplitude** is the maximum vertical disturbance caused by a wave (i.e. its height).
- **Wavelength** is the distance between corresponding points on two successive disturbances.
- **Frequency** is the number of waves produced (or passing a particular point) in one second.

There are two types of wave:

1 **Transverse waves** – the pattern of disturbance is at right angles (90°) to the direction of movement.

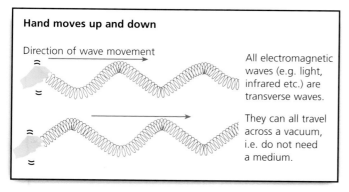

Hand moves up and down

Direction of wave movement

All electromagnetic waves (e.g. light, infrared etc.) are transverse waves.

They can all travel across a vacuum, i.e. do not need a medium.

2 **Longitudinal waves** – the pattern of disturbance is in the same direction as the direction of wave movement.

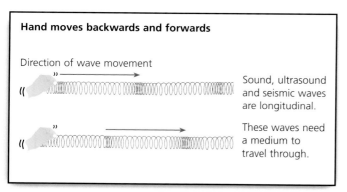

Hand moves backwards and forwards

Direction of wave movement

Sound, ultrasound and seismic waves are longitudinal.

These waves need a medium to travel through.

Similarities
- Both types of waves carry energy.

Differences
- They travel at different speeds.
- The vibrations (patterns of disturbance) are different.
- Longitudinal waves need a medium; most transverse waves (e.g. electromagnetic spectrum) do not.

Electromagnetic Waves

All energy originates from the Sun. Energy travels to the Earth in the form of **electromagnetic waves**. These waves form the **electromagnetic spectrum** in which they are ordered according to their frequency and wavelength.

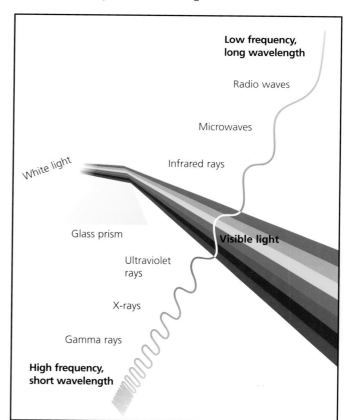

All these waves carry energy, are transverse, travel at the speed of light and can pass through a vacuum. A good mnemonic to remember the electromagnetic spectrum in order of increasing wavelength is: '**G**ood **X**ylophones **U**se **V**ery **I**nteresting **M**usical **R**hythms'.

Now You See It, Now You Don't

Electromagnetic Waves (cont.)

Electromagnetic Waves	Uses
Radio waves	Transmitting television and radio programmes between different places.
Microwaves	Satellite communication, mobile phones, cooking.
Infrared waves	Grills, toasters, heaters, remote controls, optical fibre communication, treatment of muscular problems, night vision.
Visible light	Vision, photography.
Ultraviolet waves	Fluorescent lamp and security coding, sunbeds.
X-rays	Producing shadow pictures of bones and metals.
Gamma rays	Killing cancer cells, killing bacteria on food and sterilising surgical instruments.

Dangers of Waves

Ultraviolet (UV) rays pass through the skin into the tissues. Darker skin allows less penetration and therefore more protection. The greater the amplitude the more energy the wave will carry and the more likely it is to be dangerous. Low amplitude UV is absorbed by the Earth's atmosphere.

High doses of UV rays can kill normal cells and lower doses can cause skin cancer. UV exposure also means you are more likely to develop eye cataracts.

There are three types of UV radiation:

Increasing frequency

1. **UVA** – passes through glass, penetrates deep into the skin, causes early ageing, wrinkles, DNA damage, cancer and some sunburn.
2. **UVB** – mostly absorbed by the ozone layer and the atmosphere. Dangers are the same as for UVA but also stimulates production of essential vitamin D.
3. **UVC** – almost all is absorbed by the ozone layer and the atmosphere. Most damaging.

The higher the frequency of the wave and the shorter the wavelength, the greater damage it causes. We are at most risk from UVB as almost all UVC is absorbed by the ozone layer.

Microwaves can be absorbed by the water in the cells in our body. This can cause internal heating of body tissue which may damage or kill cells. They make magnetic fields that can affect how the cells work.

Infrared rays are absorbed by the skin and felt as heat. Too much exposure will cause burns.

X-rays and **gamma rays** pass through soft tissues (although some rays are absorbed). High doses can kill normal cells and lower doses can cause cancer, through the destruction or mutation of cells.

> **HT** The higher the frequency of the waves, the more damage they can cause with excessive exposure. Gamma rays have the highest frequency, and radio waves have the lowest frequency.

Now You See It, Now You Don't

Wave Technology in Society

Much of today's technology is based on waves, for example, mobile phones. While mobile phones have many benefits, some studies have linked their use with brain tumours and cancer. Mobile phones do warm the brain slightly but it is not by as much as would result from vigorous exercise. Because mobile phones are a recent innovation, there have not been any long-term studies on the possible consequences to health.

Benefits

- Convenient method of communication.
- Easy way to stay in contact wherever you are.
- Can help in solving crime as mobile phones can be tracked.
- Scientific evidence suggests mobile phone radiation is unlikely to harm the general population.

Problems

- It is too early to be certain of the effects, as health problems may take some time to develop.
- Some people may be at higher risk because of genetic factors.
- Children may be more vulnerable because their nervous system is still developing, and with a thinner skull there may be a greater absorption of energy in the tissues in the brain.

People have concerns about health risks from the radiation from mobile phone masts as well as from the phones themselves. The media often reports on residents objecting to the proposed site of a mast, due to the potential health risks.

Phone masts are designed to give out radiation: they radiate powers of up to 100W (mobile phones radiate up to 0.25W). Some people claim that these emissions interfere with electrical signals in the body, causing headaches, dizziness and even cancer.

Exposure to microwave radiation from a mast when standing underneath it is less than from a phone. When you are close to a mast the phone sends a weaker signal. This means less energy is needed so less radiation will penetrate your head. Therefore, living in remote areas away from a mast could, theoretically, be more dangerous to mobile users, than living close to one.

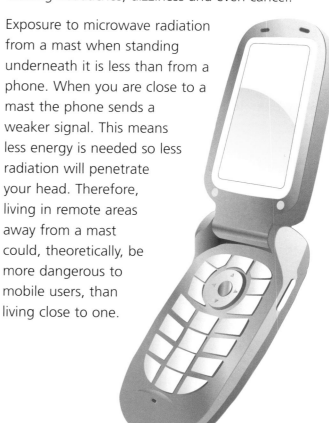

Phone mast

15–50m

Microwave beam

50–300m

Now You See It, Now You Don't

Scanning by Absorption

X-Rays to see Bone Fractures

The area with the suspected fracture is placed in front of a photographic plate and is exposed to X-rays. The X-rays are absorbed by the bone, however, they pass through the fracture and expose the photographic plate, clearly showing where the fracture is.

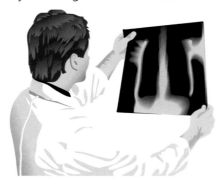

Microwaves to Monitor Rain

Microwaves have a wavelength suitable for absorption by water molecules. Satellites are able to monitor how the microwaves are absorbed by the atmosphere, showing areas of probable high rainfall.

UV to Detect Forged Bank Notes

If paper is exposed to UV light, some is absorbed. The paper and inks then emit visible light (fluorescence). Different papers and inks fluoresce differently, which can help in detecting forgeries. Security marker-pens, which glow under UV light, can be used to mark property.

Scanning by Emission

Infrared Sensors

Infrared sensors can detect temperature differences of surfaces because the higher the temperature, the more infrared radiation is emitted. Police helicopters use infrared sensors to follow suspects at night, or when the suspect hides somewhere like woodland. Rescuers can detect infrared radiation from people trapped in collapsed buildings.

Scanning by Reflection

Iris Recognition (Visible Light)

The iris in each individual eye has unique patterns so it can be photographed and stored on a computer. Later, it can be scanned with low-intensity light and the patterns from the reflected light are checked against the stored image. This is a very accurate and secure system which will be used a lot more in the future.

Ultrasound

Ultrasonic waves are sound waves (see p.85), rather than light waves. They are used in medicine to produce visual images of different parts of the body (e.g. the heart and liver) to detect problems.

Ultrasound waves are used for foetus scanning in pregnant women, to determine size and position, and to detect any abnormalities. It is safe, with no risk to patient or baby, unlike X-rays.

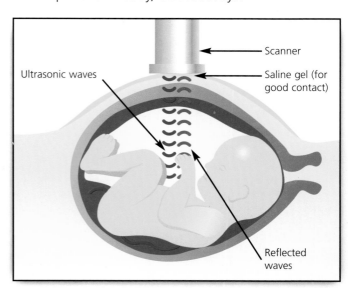

Scanner

Ultrasonic waves

Saline gel (for good contact)

Reflected waves

Now You See It, Now You Don't

Sound

Sound is produced when something vibrates backwards and forwards. Sound waves are longitudinal, travel at the speed of sound and cannot pass through a vacuum.

A sound can be heard if it is within the audible range that our ears can detect. Most humans can hear sounds in the range of 20 to 20 000 hertz (i.e. 20 to 20 000 vibrations per second).

Ultrasound waves have frequencies greater than 20 000 hertz. They are made by electronic systems which produce electrical oscillations, used to generate ultrasonic waves. Ultrasonic waves are used in medicine: they are sent into the body by the scanner which is placed in good contact with the skin. The waves are partly reflected at any surfaces or boundaries within the body which have a different density or structure, therefore highlighting any problems.

Analogue Versus Digital

Analogue signals vary continuously in amplitude and / or frequency. Your voice is an analogue signal because it is a sound wave with many different levels of loudness (amplitude) and pitch (frequency).

Digital signals do not vary. The amplitude is sampled (measured) at regular intervals (fractions of a second). These sampled measurements are then turned into a digital code called **binary** (0s and 1s).

Analogue Signals

Digital Signals

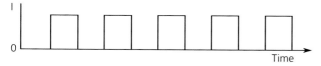

Advantages of Using Digital Signals

- There is no loss in quality: the sequence of 0s and 1s will not change. (Analogue signals lose quality.)
- More information can be transmitted per second.
- There is no change in the signal information during transmission. If noise (interference) is added during transmission, a regenerator restores the pulses. (Analogue signals cannot be cleaned up: if they are amplified the interference is amplified too.)
- They can be handled by microprocessors (as in computers).
- Several signals can be sent along the same cable at the same time.

Digital Technology

CDs and DVDs have a metal layer with millions of tiny bumps arranged in a spiral pattern. When a disc is rotated, laser light is reflected from the bumps. The reflected pulses (0s or 1s) are turned into electrical signals and then decoded to produce the sound. Digital technology has had a huge impact on the music industry:

- music keyboards can be connected to computers
- CDs and DVDs have replaced vinyl, cassettes and video tapes (analogue) as the main systems
- music can be downloaded from the Internet
- instruments can be synthesised
- music can be compressed (resulting in less required storage space and reducing the product size) and played on MP3 players
- digital radio – DAB (digital audio broadcasting).

Now You See It, Now You Don't

Refraction and Reflection

When a ray of visible or infrared light travels from glass, perspex or water into air, some light is also reflected from the boundary. The amount of light that is reflected depends on the size of the angle of incidence in relation to the critical angle.

Normally when a ray of visible or infrared light passes into air it is refracted away from the normal. This happens if the angle of incidence is less than the critical angle.

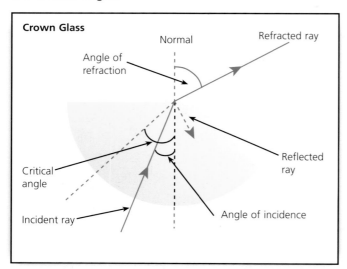

Crown Glass

Normal — Refracted ray — Angle of refraction — Critical angle — Incident ray — Reflected ray — Angle of incidence

However, if the angle of incidence is greater than the critical angle…

- no light is **refracted** (bent away from the glass, perspex or water)
- all light is **reflected** at the boundary.

This is **total internal reflection.**

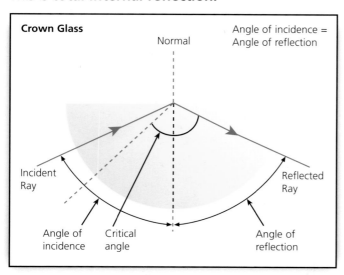

Crown Glass

Normal — Angle of incidence = Angle of reflection — Incident Ray — Reflected Ray — Angle of incidence — Critical angle — Angle of reflection

The density of the material will influence the critical angle.

Material	Critical angle with air (°)	Physical Density (kg/m³)
Ice	50	920
Water	49	1 000
Perspex	42	1 190
Crown Glass	41	2 600
Diamond	24	3 300

The speed of a light wave is dependent upon the properties of the medium. In the case of an electromagnetic wave, the wave speed depends upon the **optical density** of that material. The optical density of a material relates to the material's ability to absorb the energy of an electromagnetic wave. The more optically dense a material is, the slower a wave will move through the material.

Optical Fibres

The use of **optical fibres** enables the transmission of large amounts of information over greater distances at quicker speeds; the information is carried on light waves making use of total internal reflection. An optical fibre is a long, flexible, transparent cable of very small diameter. Light is totally internally reflected along its length, staying inside the fibre, until it emerges at the other end.

Advantages of Optical Fibres over Conventional Electrical Cables
- They are thinner: they take up less space, and there can be more cables within one outer protective sleeve.
- They are lighter and easier to transport and lay.
- They carry more signals.
- They are not affected by electrical interference.
- They cannot be 'tapped'.
- There is less need for frequent amplification along the cable due to loss of signal strength.

Now You See It, Now You Don't

Wave Speed

Wave speed, frequency and wavelength are related by the equation:

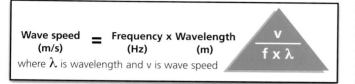

Wave speed = Frequency x Wavelength
(m/s)   (Hz)   (m)
where λ is wavelength and v is wave speed

$\dfrac{v}{f \times \lambda}$

Example 1

A sound wave has a frequency of 168Hz and a wavelength of 2m. What is the speed of sound?

Wave speed = **frequency x wavelength**
= 168Hz x 2m
= **336m/s**

Example 2

Radio 5 Live transmits on a frequency of 909kHz. If the speed of radio waves is 300 000 000m/s what is the wavelength of the waves?

Wavelength $= \dfrac{\textbf{wave speed}}{\textbf{frequency}} = \dfrac{300\,000\,000\text{m/s}}{909\,000\text{Hz}}$
= **330m**

Speed

Speed, distance travelled and time taken are related by the equation:

Speed (m/s) $= \dfrac{\textbf{Distance travelled (m)}}{\textbf{Time taken (s)}}$

$\dfrac{d}{s \times t}$

Example: Echo Sounding

Ultrasonic waves are sent out from the bottom of a ship. The time delay of the reflections can be used to calculate the depth of the water.

How deep is the sea if it takes 0.5s for the wave to travel from the transmitter to the receiver?
The speed of sound in water = 1400m/s.

d = **s x t**
= 1400 x 0.5 = **700m**

depth of sea $= \dfrac{700}{2}$ = **350m**

> Total distance travelled – wave has travelled to seabed and back

Earthquakes and Tsunami Waves

The Earth's surface is split into several large tectonic plates, which are moving slowly (a few centimetres per year). It is the movement of these plates that causes **earthquakes**.

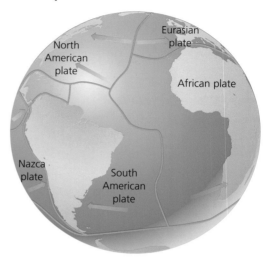

North American plate
Eurasian plate
African plate
Nazca plate
South American plate

A **tsunami**, or tidal wave, is caused by an underwater disturbance, normally an earthquake or volcano. The wave travels fast, has a long wavelength and is low, and stores vast amounts of energy. As it approaches land, the height of the wave increases drastically and it transfers the energy to everything in its way.

HT It is very difficult to predict when earthquakes and, therefore, tsunamis will occur. Scientists have been trying for hundreds of years. They can predict where they will happen, as they know where the faults in the Earth's crust are, but not *when* they will happen. This is because the Earth's tectonic plates do not move in regular patterns. Scientists can measure the strain on underground rocks to evaluate the likelihood of a forthcoming earthquake, but they cannot predict an exact time.

Although we are not able to predict individual earthquakes, the world's largest earthquakes do have a spatial pattern, and estimates of the locations and magnitudes of some future large earthquakes can now be made.

Now You See It, Now You Don't

Seismic Waves and the Structure of the Earth

Seismic waves are vibrations in the Earth which can cause massive destruction. The paths they follow and their speed of travel provide evidence of the Earth's layered structure. When an earthquake occurs two types of seismic wave are generated.

Primary Waves (P waves)

Primary waves occur first.

Primary waves are longitudinal waves: the ground is made to vibrate in the same direction as the wave is travelling, i.e. up and down. They can travel through solids and liquids and through all layers of the Earth.

Secondary Waves (S waves)

Secondary waves occur second, because they travel more slowly that P waves.

Secondary waves are transverse waves: the ground is made to vibrate at right angles to the direction the wave is travelling, i.e. from left to right. They can travel through solids but not liquids. They cannot travel through the Earth's outer core and are slower than primary waves.

A study of seismic waves indicates that the Earth is made up of…
- a thin crust
- a mantle which is semi-fluid and extends almost halfway to the centre
- a core which is over half of the Earth's diameter with a liquid outer part and a solid inner part.

As primary waves are the only type of wave to reach the opposite side of the Earth and can travel through a liquid, this provides good evidence that the outer core of the Earth is liquid.

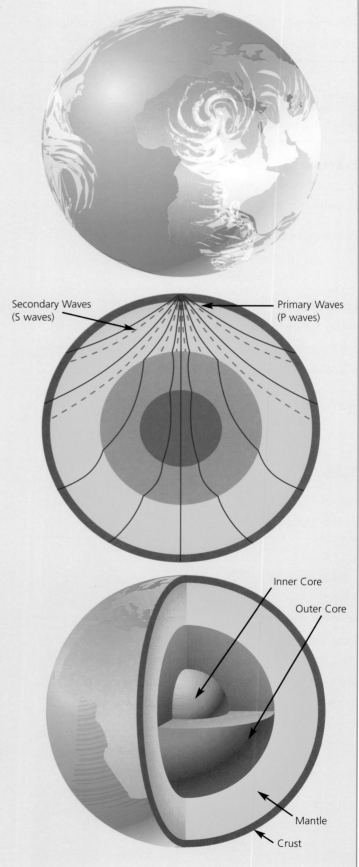

Secondary Waves (S waves)

Primary Waves (P waves)

Inner Core

Outer Core

Mantle

Crust

Now You See It, Now You Don't

Glossary

Absorption – a substance's ability to absorb energy, e.g. UV into the skin

Amplitude – the maximum vertical disturbance caused by a wave

Analogue – a signal that varies continuously in amplitude and/or frequency

Digital – a signal that uses a binary code (0s and 1s) to represent information

Electromagnetic spectrum – a continuous arrangement that displays electromagnetic waves in order of increasing frequency or wavelength

Emission – the outflow of electromagnetic radiation from a system

Fluorescent – the emission of light by a substance which has been exposed to electromagnetic radiation

Frequency – the number of complete wave oscillations per second, or the number of complete waves to pass a point in 1 second. Measured in hertz (Hz)

Gamma rays – high frequency electromagnetic waves with a short wavelength that can damage and kill cells

Infrared – a region of the electromagnetic spectrum just below the red end of the visible spectrum

Longitudinal – an energy-carrying wave in which the movement of the particles is in line with the direction in which the energy is being transferred

Microwave – a region of the electromagnetic spectrum between infrared and radio waves

Mutation – a change in the genetic material of a cell (or virus)

Optical fibres – very thin strands of pure optical glass or plastic that use totally internally reflected light to carry information

Radiation – the process of transferring energy by electromagnetic waves

Reflection – the deflection of a ray of light when it hits the boundary between two different surfaces, e.g. air and glass, as in a mirror

Refraction – the phenomenon that occurs when a wave passes from one medium into another, causing a change in speed and direction (unless the wave hits the second medium at right angles)

Scanning – the act of moving across a surface and applying the same experimental technique at each point, e.g. scanning the intensities of parts of a visual image, as in iris recognition

Transverse – a wave in which the oscillations (vibrations) are at 90° to the direction of energy transfer

Ultrasound – sound waves with frequencies above the upper limit of human hearing, i.e. above 20 000 Hz

Ultraviolet – a region of the electromagnetic spectrum between X-rays and visible light

Vacuum – a volume of space that has no particles in it at all

Wave – a moving disturbance that is able to carry energy

Wave speed – (measured in m/s) found by multiplying the frequency (Hz) by the wavelength (m) or by dividing the distance travelled (m) by the time taken (s)

Wavelength – the distance between two successive points on a wave which are at the same stage of oscillation, i.e. the distance between two successive peaks

X-rays – a region of the electromagnetic spectrum between gamma rays and ultraviolet rays. X-rays can be emitted when a solid target is bombarded with electrons

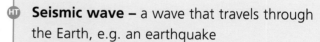 **Seismic wave –** a wave that travels through the Earth, e.g. an earthquake

Space and its Mysteries

The Solar System

The **Solar System** is made up of the **Sun** (a star) and the nine **planets** which surround it. These planets move around the Sun in paths called **orbits**, which are slightly elliptical (squashed circles).

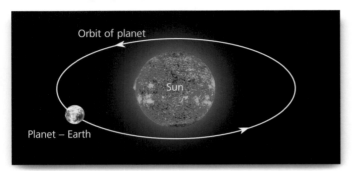

Planet	Diameter (km)	Distance from Sun (million km)
Mercury	4 880	58
Venus	12 112	107.5
Earth	12 742	149.6
Mars	6 790	228
Jupiter	142 600	778
Saturn	120 200	1 427
Uranus	49 000	2 870
Neptune	50 000	4 497
*Pluto	2 284	5 900

- The Sun is a continuous source of light and other forms of electromagnetic radiation. We can only see the other planets because light from the Sun is reflected off them to us.
- The position of the other planets as seen from the Earth changes as they and the Earth orbit the Sun.
- The Earth takes one year (365 ¼ days) to orbit the Sun once.
- The average surface temperature of the Earth stays fairly constant due to the presence of the atmosphere.
- Mercury and Venus take less time to orbit the Sun as they don't have as far to travel. Their surface temperatures are greater than the Earth's since they are closer to the Sun. Venus is hotter than Mars because of its dense atmosphere.
- Mars, Jupiter, Saturn, Uranus, Neptune and *Pluto take more time to orbit the Sun as they have further to travel. Their surface temperatures are lower than the Earth's since they are further away from the Sun.
- Stars emit light and planets reflect light.
- Our Moon orbits the Earth at a distance of 380 000km.

*Pluto is now classed as a 'dwarf planet'.

Stars, Galaxies and the Universe

Our Sun is one of many billions of stars in the **Milky Way**. The Milky Way is just one **galaxy** of many millions of galaxies in the Universe.

Not to scale

Our Sun

Our Sun

Our galaxy the Milky Way

Our galaxy

The Universe

Measuring the Universe

A **light year** is the distance travelled by light in one Earth year. It is equal to 9 500 000 000 000km (light travels at 300 000km/s).

The Earth in Space

Our planet, Earth, has sufficient gravity to hold us firmly to its surface, and contains all the resources we need to live. The gravity is even strong enough (unlike on the Moon) to hold individual gas particles, so we have an atmosphere. It rotates providing day and night. We have seasons because the Earth's axis is tilted. The northern hemisphere, including Britain, is tilted towards the Sun in summer and is tilted away in winter.

We define space as beginning where the Earth's atmosphere ends: 100km from the Earth's surface. At this distance, the atmosphere is very thin. However, gravity (from the Earth) does not end at 100km. An astronaut's weight will only have fallen by 3% at 100km from the Earth. Even at an altitude of 2600km, gravity is still 50% of its value on Earth.

Weightlessness

When astronauts travel to the Moon they leave the Earth's **gravitational field** but they are influenced by the Moon's weaker gravitational field. Astronauts are weightless as they move away from the Earth.

Astronauts orbiting the Earth are not weightless because they are still under the influence of the Earth's gravity. But they do experience **weightlessness** because, as a spacecraft orbits the Earth, it is, in effect, continually falling towards the Earth. The circular motion produces an outward force that balances the inward pull of gravity (i.e. the forces balance and the astronaut experiences weightlessness, similar to a free-fall parachutist). If there were no Earth gravity, the orbiting spacecraft would fly off into space.

Space and its Mysteries

Mass and Weight

- **Mass** is a measure of how much material there is in an object. The units are grams (g) and kilograms (kg)
- **Weight** is a measure of the force exerted on a mass due to the pull of gravity. The units are newtons (N).

If you went to the Moon, your mass would be the same as it is on Earth, but your weight would be less (due to a smaller gravitational force).

On Earth		On the Moon	
Mass (kg)	Weight (N)	Mass (kg)	Weight (N)
1	10	1	1.67
2	20	2	3.34
5	50	5	8.35
10	100	10	16.7

Gravitational Field Strength

Gravitational field strength is measured in newtons per kilogram (N/kg). On Earth the gravitational field strength is 10N/kg. On the Moon it is 1.67N/kg.

The weight of a mass in different gravitational fields can be calculated using the following equation:

$$\text{Weight (N)} = \text{Mass (kg)} \times \text{Gravitational field strength (N/kg)}$$

$$\frac{W}{m \times g}$$

Example

Calculate the weight of an object on Earth and on the Moon if it has a mass of 7kg.

Weight on Earth = 7kg x 10N/kg = **70N**
Weight on Moon = 7kg x 1.67N/kg = **11.69N**

Acceleration of Free-fall

Acceleration of free-fall refers to the greatest acceleration that a mass can achieve when it falls in a gravitational field. It is measured in metres per second per second (m/s²). Acceleration of free-fall has the same value as gravitational field strength – it just uses different units. This means it can also be used as a value for g in the equation for calculating weight:

$$\text{Weight (N)} = \text{Mass (kg)} \times \text{Acceleration of Free Fall (m/s}^2\text{)}$$

$$\frac{W}{m \times g}$$

where g is acceleration of free-fall

This is a specific version of the general equation used to calculate force (see below).

Force, Mass and Acceleration

Force, mass and acceleration are related by the following equation:

$$\text{Force (N)} = \text{Mass (kg)} \times \text{Acceleration (m/s}^2\text{)}$$

$$\frac{F}{m \times a}$$

This equation can be rearranged to predict how an object will behave.

Example

If toy car of mass 800g is accelerated by a force of 0.4N, what will be the rate of acceleration?

$$\text{Acceleration} = \frac{\text{Force}}{\text{Mass}} = \frac{0.4N}{0.8kg} = \textbf{0.5m/s}^2$$

Mass must be in kilograms

Space and its Mysteries

Conditions in Space

The temperature in interplanetary space is very cold. If a thermometer in space was shielded from all the Sun's radiation it would read about -270°C. The temperature depends on the distance from the Sun. At the Earth's distance, it would be 7°C. (The Earth is, on average, warmer than this because the atmosphere holds the heat in.)

In interplanetary space, there is no air and the gravitational force is zero: this is why astronauts experience weightlessness.

HT These conditions can be partly allowed for in spacecrafts:

- The spacecraft rolls constantly to ensure even Sun exposure. If it did not roll, one side (facing the Sun) would become very hot, whilst the shaded side would be very cold. Unequal Sun exposure could crack wires and pipes, and any liquids on the cold side would freeze.

- Astronauts take all the required oxygen with them. Oxygen is needed for breathing, and conventional jet engines need oxygen to burn fuel. In the future, plants could be used as an oxygen source (due to photosynthesis) for long journeys (e.g. to Mars).

- The lack of gravity means that the muscles in the body do not need to work as hard as they do on Earth. To reduce muscle wastage, astronauts must exercise for at least two hours a day on special exercise machines on board the spacecrafts.

- To overcome the weightlessness problems, scientists are working on spinning the spacecraft to make its own **artificial gravity**.

Scientists are trying to find ways to overcome the problems of long space flights, most of which are caused by reduced gravity and radiation from the Sun.

In space, astronauts' body fluid is redistributed with less in the legs and more in the face. Scientists have designed special trousers which have air pumped into them to fit tightly and help keep fluid in the legs.

The heart does not need to work as hard in space because it does not need to work against gravity to pump blood. This could cause heart attacks on return to Earth. Astronauts' bones are also likely to deteriorate in space. To reduce these risks, astronauts must exercise daily.

Radiation

Astronauts are exposed to harmful **radiation** whilst in space. The Sun emits a lot of harmful radiation, especially during solar storms. The Earth's atmosphere and magnetic field shield us from most of these, but in space, other types of shielding are needed. Water is an effective shield, so scientists are looking at the possibility of surrounding spacecrafts with water tanks. Electrostatic fields may also be used.

Space and its Mysteries

Spacecraft: Action and Reaction

In terms of forces, every action has an equal and opposite reaction: if you push against something and it does not move, it pushes back with an equal and opposite force. If the forces do not balance, there will be motion in the direction of the largest force.

Spacecraft engines rely on this principle; the engines push air backwards (**action**), and the air reacts by pushing the spacecraft forwards (**reaction**), thrusting it through the atmosphere.

To move forward, the reaction must be larger than the action. However, whilst in the Earth's atmosphere, a spacecraft also needs to exert enough force to overcome the pull of gravity. This is possible using powerful rocket engines which act on the plentiful supply of air in the atmosphere.

When the spacecraft enters space, there is no gravity so less force is required. However, there is no air either, so spacecraft must generate gas to achieve the same effect. To do this they carry materials, referred to as 'reaction mass', into space with them. These are reacted together to produce hot gases, which are forced through small thrust engines on the outside of the spacecraft, propelling it along. If it runs out of reaction mass, it cannot manoeuvre.

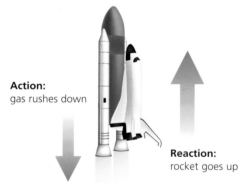

Action: gas rushes down

Reaction: rocket goes up

Gravity

When something is thrown into the air, it falls back down due to the Earth's gravitational pull. To escape the Earth's pull it must be thrown very fast. This is called the **escape velocity**. Escape velocity increases with planet mass and decreases with radius. So a small, dense planet (high mass) will have a high escape velocity.

Black Holes

The smallest and most dense known object is a **black hole**, which has an escape velocity of more than the speed of light. Anything that approaches a black hole will be pulled in by the huge gravitational pull. Black holes even bend light which passes close enough to be influenced by its gravitational field. This has an impact on astronomy because light from distant stars and galaxies may have been bent, giving false information on where they actually are.

Benefits of Knowledge about the Universe

Through space exploration, many useful inventions have been discovered (e.g. solar cells). Over 1500 inventions are being used as a direct result of space research. Here are some examples:

- **Imaging technology:** the development of camera microchips for the Hubble telescope led to mobile phone cameras and medical advanced imaging, e.g. Digital Image Breast Biopsy and improved ultrasound scanners.
- **Satellite technology:** geostationary communication satellites allow instant news coverage, international telephone calls, the Internet and email. Satellites like 'Landstat' can monitor erosion, deforestation and ocean temperatures.
- **Weather forecasting:** satellites like 'Meteostat' give a continuous view of weather fronts which enable the prediction of the weather days in advance.
- **Handheld and car navigation systems** use satellites as well as intelligence or spy requirements.
- Smoke detectors, hang gliders, high-powered batteries, sports bras, freeze-dried food, air-traffic control systems and programmable heart pacemakers are all inventions resulting from space exploration.

Discovering Intelligent Life

There are two ways of looking for intelligent life in the Universe:

1 Sending spaceships out to collect and return data. The main problem with this is the enormous distances and journey times involved – thousands of years.

2 Searching for radio signals. Radio telescopes receive information all the time. They are better than light-collecting telescopes when looking for alien signals as light can be blocked by dust particles and gas.

The position of a planet within its solar system determines its potential for the existence of life. A planet should be within a 'habitable zone' orbiting its star (i.e. a similar distance as the Earth is from the Sun).

It is unlikely that our two nearest neighbours (Venus and Mars) will have any life. For example, Venus is too hot (its dense atmosphere gives a huge greenhouse effect) and its atmosphere would crush us.

Life on the Moons

Within our Solar System, some of the larger moons seem more likely to have life forms than the planets.

Examples:

 Titan – (Saturn's moon) has a significant atmosphere of organic-rich nitrogen, low gravity, ice, and an ocean of liquid ethane.

 Europa – (Jupiter's moon) is covered with ice and probably has water and a rocky core underneath. It also has gravity.

 Triton – (Neptune's moon) has an atmosphere and is covered with an ocean of liquid nitrogen.

Although it is possible that there are basic life forms (e.g. microorganisms) on some moons in the Solar System, we need to find other solar systems to search for intelligent life.

Conditions for Life on Other Planets

A star must pass five tests before its planets can be classed as potential homes to extraterrestrial life.

1 It must be on the **main sequence**. When stars fuse hydrogen into helium, generating light and heat, they are in a stable state known as the main sequence. Hydrogen is abundant in stars, so most stay on the main sequence a long time, giving life chance to evolve.

2 It needs to be in the **right temperature** range. The hottest stars burn out and die quickly, while cooler stars may not produce enough energy to sustain life.

3 It must demonstrate **stable conditions**. The star's brightness must not vary so much that it would alternately freeze and fry any life that develops around it.

4 It must be the **right age**. The Sun is 4.6 billion years old, so life on Earth has had time to develop. The star Alpha Centauri A is older than the Sun, so life may have evolved on its planets.

5 It must have enough of the **heavy elements** (e.g. carbon, nitrogen, oxygen and iron) needed for biological life.

Space and its Mysteries

The Search for Extraterrestrial Intelligence (SETI)

Between 1990 and 2005, 130 stars with orbiting planets were found, and the first image was produced in 2004. Scientists used other evidence like changes in brightness as the planets orbited, and a 'wobble' in the star's motion caused by the planets' gravity. Planets around stars are called exoplanets.

In 1992, NASA set up **SETI**, which looks for radio signals that may have been emitted by aliens. Using SETI@home, over 50 000 people around the world are helping to process data.

Extraterrestrial Life

For
<ul><li>There have been many reported sightings.</li><li>Other life may not require the same conditions as on Earth.</li><li>The Universe is so big, there are bound to be many solar systems still undiscovered.</li></ul>
Against
<ul><li>Earth is unique, therefore life is unique.</li><li>No other known planet has the same conditions as on Earth.</li><li>Searches have never detected anything definite.</li><li>Sightings have never been proven.</li></ul>

Unmanned Space Exploration

The distances involved in exploring the Solar System, let alone exploring into the Milky Way, are huge. It would take several years for a spacecraft to travel to Pluto. It is not realistic to send manned spacecraft on such long journeys, so data logging and remote sensing is required where information can be sent to receivers on Earth via radio waves.

Unmanned crafts are often used in space exploration because…
- they are safer
- the journey is so long
- the equipment is equally as effective (or more so) than humans (e.g. collecting soil / rock from a planet or moon surface and performing an analysis).

Examples of unmanned spacecraft:
- **Viking Lander** (1975) took images of the surface of Mars and analysed the atmosphere and soil.
- **NASA Spirit and Opportunity Rover** is currently investigating Mars.

Viking Lander

NASA Spirit and Opportunity Rover

Theories of the Universe

Steady State Theory: many people used to believe that the Universe had no beginning and would never end. Few believe in this theory now.

Big Bang Theory: it is now thought that the Universe started about 15 million years ago when a massively dense object experienced a tremendous explosion known as the Big Bang. Since then the Universe has been continually expanding.

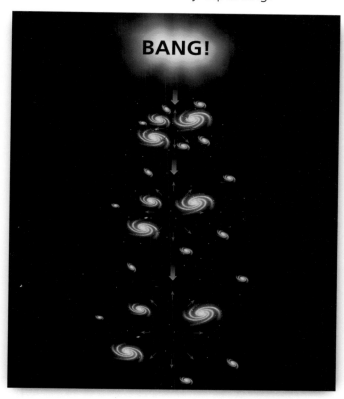

BANG!

There are three theories on the future of the Universe. They all depend upon how much matter there is in the Universe:

1. As the amount of matter increases, gravitational forces will become stronger, slowing the **expansion** of the Universe down and starting to pull the matter back together; this is called the 'big crunch'. There could then be another big bang. This expanding and collapsing Universe is called the **oscillating theory**.

2. If there is not enough matter the Universe will expand forever.

3. If there is just the right amount of matter the Universe will reach a certain fixed size.

Evidence for the Big Bang Theory

Studies of light from distant galaxies show that they are moving away from us (i.e. the Universe is expanding). Light from these galaxies is 'shifted' towards the red part of the visible spectrum; this is known as **red shift**.

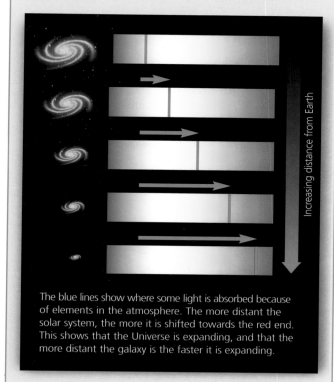

Increasing distance from Earth

The blue lines show where some light is absorbed because of elements in the atmosphere. The more distant the solar system, the more it is shifted towards the red end. This shows that the Universe is expanding, and that the more distant the galaxy is the faster it is expanding.

- Large amounts of light elements like hydrogen and helium have been detected throughout the Universe.
- Cosmic microwaves have been detected. These prove that the Universe is cooling (i.e. it started very hot and is cooling as it expands).
- The oldest stars are younger than the Universe.

Dark Matter

All the theories depend on an accurate calculation of the mass in the Universe. Scientists have discovered that about 90% of the mass cannot be accounted for with known objects like stars and galaxies. This 'missing' mass is called **dark matter**.

Space and its Mysteries

Asteroids and Comets

Asteroids are a band of rock debris found between the orbits of Mars and Jupiter.

Comets have a core of frozen gas and dust. As they approach the Sun gases evaporate to form the tail making the comet easy to see.

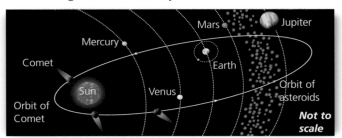

Many small asteroids collide with the Earth each year. The chances of a catastrophic collision (from an asteroid or comet) are very small but a 1–10km wide asteroid is predicted to hit the Earth within the next million years. The impact and tidal waves could be devastating and the resulting dust will fill the atmosphere, preventing light and heat from reaching Earth. Plants and animals would die due to lack of light for photosynthesis and the very low temperatures. A large comet collision could have the same effects.

The Life and Death of a Star

Stars are all at different stages in their life cycles. They do not last forever, and some stars we can see will no longer exist; it takes 4.3 years for the light from the closest star to reach Earth and thousands of years for the more distant stars. Our Sun is a small-to-average sized star.

Star Formation

Stars are made from **nebula** (clouds of gases and dust) that are pulled together, or collapsed, by gravitational forces. This increases the temperature, and nuclear reactions start to take place, releasing massive amounts of energy and forming a star. Eventually the required hydrogen gas runs out, causing the star to expand and get colder. What happens next depends upon the size of the star.

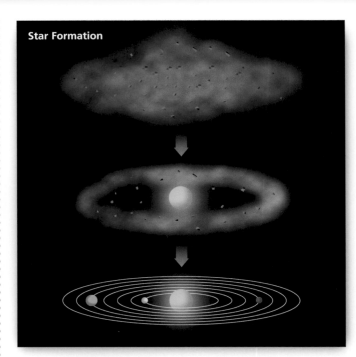

A star the size of the Sun becomes a **red giant**. It continues to cool before collapsing under its own gravity to become a **white dwarf**, then a **black dwarf**:

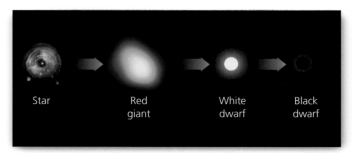

A star much bigger than the Sun becomes a **red supergiant**. It shrinks rapidly and explodes, releasing massive amounts of energy, dust and gas into space. This is a **supernova**. The dust and gas (nebula) will form new stars and the remains of the supernova will be either a **neutron star** or a **black hole**:

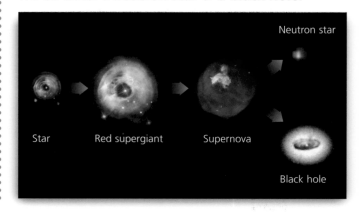

Space and its Mysteries

Glossary

Acceleration – the rate of change of velocity of a body

Action – a force that is exerted on something

Asteroid – a piece of rock debris from the asteroid belt between Mars and Jupiter

Atmosphere – a mass of gases surrounding a planet

Big Bang – the rapid expansion of material at an extremely high density; the event believed by many scientists to have been the start of the Universe

Comet – an interplanetary body with a nucleus of dust and ice

Extraterrestrial – outside the Earth and its atmosphere

Galaxy – a group of millions of stars held together by gravitational forces

Gravitational field – the area around an object where gravitational effects are felt

Gravity – a force that acts between two bodies

Interplanetary – the area between planets. It contains electromagnetic radiation, solar wind, cosmic rays, microscopic dust particles and magnetic fields

Mass – a measure of how much matter an object contains

Nebula – a faint mass of gaseous matter found outside our Solar System

Orbit – the path that a satellite takes around a larger object (a planet is a satellite of the Sun)

Oscillating theory – the theory that the expansion of the Universe will eventually slow down and stop. This motion will then be reversed, resulting in the 'big crunch' with all matter concentrated into a small volume with a very high density

Planet – a major body orbiting the Sun or another star

Radiation – energy in the form of a wave which needs no medium to carry it, e.g. light and radio waves

Reaction – the equal and opposite of action, e.g. as you are sitting, the action is your weight on the seat; the seat supports you by pushing back with an equal and opposite force (the reaction)

SETI – Search for Extraterrestrial Intelligence: a scientific experiment with Internet-connected computers collecting data

Star – a large gaseous body that radiates light and other electromagnetic radiations, and produces energy by nuclear fusion

Steady state theory – the theory that the Universe appears the same from all positions at all times. It relies on the production of new matter in the spaces between galaxies

Stellar – relating to a star / stars

Sun – the star closest to the Earth; the centre of our Solar System

Temperature – a measure of the relative 'hotness' of a body. It depends upon the average kinetic energy of the particles, measured in °C

Universe – everything that exists as matter and the space in which it is found

Weight – the gravitational force acting on a body

Weightlessness – when no weight is felt; where no gravitational force is acting

---

HT

Black hole – a body in the Universe with such a large gravitational strength that even light cannot escape; formed at the end of the life cycle of a massive star

Dark matter – up to 90% of the Universe. Evidence for its existence is measured by gravitational effects rather than by visible observation

Red shift – light from the distant edges of the Universe is moved (or shifted) towards the red part of the visible spectrum. This shows the Universe is expanding or moving away from the Earth

Index

Index

Acknowledgements

The authors and publisher would like to thank everyone who contributed images to this book:

IFC	©iStockphoto.com / Andrei Tchernov
p.28	©iStockphoto.com / Lisa McDonald
p.28	©iStockphoto.com (tablets)
p.29	©iStockphoto.com (bacteria)
p.29	©iStockphoto.com (fungi)
p.29	©iStockphoto.com / Konstantinos Kokkinis
p.29	©iStockphoto.com / Matthew Cole
p.30	©iStockphoto.com (skin)
p.32	©iStockphoto.com (TB)
p.57	©iStockphoto.com / Todd Harrison
p.58	©iStockphoto.com / Chronis Chamalidis
p.61	©iStockphoto.com / Paul IJsendoorn
p.61	©iStockphoto.com / Jami Garrison
p.61	©iStockphoto.com / Todd Harrison
p.63	©iStockphoto.com (oscilloscope)
p.83	©iStockphoto.com / Brandon Laufenberg
p.84	©iStockphoto.com (satellite)
p.84	©iStockphoto.com / Dawn Hudson
p.85	©iStockphoto.com (MP3)
p.90	©iStockphoto.com / George Argyropoulos
p.92	©iStockphoto.com / George Argyropoulos
p.93	©iStockphoto.com / Stephen Sweet
p.94	©iStockphoto.com / Matthew Cole
p.95	NASA
p.95	©iStockphoto.com / Michael Puerzer
p.96	NASA
p.98	NASA

ISBN 1-905129-63-7

Published by Lonsdale, a division of Huveaux Plc.

Authors: Aleksander Jedrosz
Susan Loxley
John Watts

Project Editor: Katie Smith

Editor: Rebecca Skinner

Cover and concept design: Sarah Duxbury

Designer: Anne-Marie Taylor

Artwork: HL Studios

Notes

Periodic Table

Key

1 ← Mass number	
H hydrogen	
1 ← Atomic number (Proton number)	

Group 1	Group 2											Group 3	Group 4	Group 5	Group 6	Group 7	Group 8 or 0
																	4 **He** helium 2
7 **Li** lithium 3	9 **Be** beryllium 4											11 **B** boron 5	12 **C** carbon 6	14 **N** nitrogen 7	16 **O** oxygen 8	19 **F** fluorine 9	20 **Ne** neon 10
23 **Na** sodium 11	24 **Mg** magnesium 12											27 **Al** aluminium 13	28 **Si** silicon 14	31 **P** phosphorus 15	32 **S** sulphur 16	35 **Cl** chlorine 17	40 **Ar** argon 18
39 **K** potassium 19	40 **Ca** calcium 20	45 **Sc** scandium 21	48 **Ti** titanium 22	51 **V** vanadium 23	52 **Cr** chromium 24	55 **Mn** manganese 25	56 **Fe** iron 26	59 **Co** cobalt 27	59 **Ni** nickel 28	63 **Cu** copper 29	64 **Zn** zinc 30	70 **Ga** gallium 31	73 **Ge** germanium 32	75 **As** arsenic 33	79 **Se** selenium 34	80 **Br** bromine 35	84 **Kr** krypton 36
85 **Rb** rubidium 37	88 **Sr** strontium 38	89 **Y** yttrium 39	91 **Zr** zirconium 40	93 **Nb** niobium 41	96 **Mo** molybdenum 42	98 **Tc** technetium 43	101 **Ru** ruthenium 44	103 **Rh** rhodium 45	106 **Pd** palladium 46	108 **Ag** silver 47	112 **Cd** cadmium 48	115 **In** indium 49	119 **Sn** tin 50	122 **Sb** antimony 51	128 **Te** tellurium 52	127 **I** iodine 53	131 **Xe** xenon 54
133 **Cs** caesium 55	137 **Ba** barium 56	139 **La** lanthanum 57	178 **Hf** hafnium 72	181 **Ta** tantalum 73	184 **W** tungsten 74	186 **Re** rhenium 75	190 **Os** osmium 76	192 **Ir** iridium 77	195 **Pt** platinum 78	197 **Au** gold 79	201 **Hg** mercury 80	204 **Tl** thallium 81	207 **Pb** lead 82	209 **Bi** bismuth 83	210 **Po** polonium 84	210 **At** astatine 85	222 **Rn** radon 86
223 **Fr** francium 87	226 **Ra** radium 88	227 **Ac** actinium 89															

140 **Ce** cerium 58	141 **Pr** praseodymium 59	144 **Nd** neodymium 60	147 **Pm** promethium 61	150 **Sm** samarium 62	152 **Eu** europium 63	157 **Gd** gadolinium 64	159 **Tb** terbium 65	162 **Dy** dysprosium 66	165 **Ho** holmium 67	167 **Er** erbium 68	169 **Tm** thulium 69	173 **Yb** ytterbium 70	175 **Lu** lutetium 71
232 **Th** thorium 90	231 **Pa** protactinium 91	238 **U** uranium 92	237 **Np** neptunium 93	242 **Pu** plutonium 94	243 **Am** americium 95	247 **Cm** curium 96	247 **Bk** berkelium 97	251 **Cf** californium 98	254 **Es** einsteinium 99	253 **Fm** fermium 100	256 **Md** mendelevium 101	254 **No** nobelium 102	257 **Lw** lawrencium 103

→ The lines of elements going across are called periods.

→ The columns of elements going down are called groups.